The Beauty and Glory
of the Last Things

The Beauty and Glory
of the Last Things

Edited by
Joel R. Beeke

Reformation Heritage Books
Grand Rapids, Michigan

The Beauty and Glory of the Last Things
Copyright © 2019 Puritan Reformed Theological Seminary

Published by
Reformation Heritage Books
2965 Leonard St. NE
Grand Rapids, MI 49525
616-977-0889
e-mail: orders@heritagebooks.org
website: www.heritagebooks.org

Printed in the United States of America
19 20 21 22 23/10 9 8 7 6 5 4 3 2 1

ISBN: 978-1-60178-706-4 (hardback)
ISBN: 978-1-60178-707-1 (e-pub)

*For additional Reformed literature, request a free book list
from Reformation Heritage Books at the above address.*

With heartfelt appreciation for

Ronald Kalifungwa and **Conrad Mbewe**

dear Zambian brothers and good friends,
able preachers and pastors,
and former speakers at the PRTS Conference.

—JRB

Contents

Contents

Preface

We live in a challenging cultural moment; there are reasons for great alarm and concern in society around us and it's easy to lose heart. We are daily surrounded by the ugly and the unthinkable, by the vain and the vanishing. We dare not join the world in its discordant anthem of rebellion against God—in the evil thoughts, words, and actions of a self-asserting, fallen humanity. Yet even as we say "no" to ungodliness, we cannot avoid being stung by the discouragement of living in a fallen world. The Christian hope of the last things, so wonderfully disclosed in the Scriptures and so certainly embodied in our risen Savior, is a beacon of beauty and glory shining on our way as we traverse the ugly and the gloomy.

Suffice it to say that there are few things more important than the theme of the last things for faithfully living the Christian life: Nothing fills the Christian's heart with more joy than the anticipation of seeing Christ face to face and joining Him in His eternal glory. Sadly, there are few themes more abused, misunderstood, and misapplied by believer and unbeliever alike. What are the signs of the last times and what do they mean? What will heaven be like? How does the Bible describe hell? These questions require biblically-informed, practical, and reverent treatment, especially in the face of a kaleidoscope of far-flung opinions the world presents us with. There is a heaven that awaits; there is a hell that we must flee; there is a victory of Christ in the world by the gospel.

At the Puritan Reformed Conference held in August 2019, we glimpsed afresh the beauty and glory of the last things. We benefited greatly from the combined wisdom and experience of professors and ministers who have unfolded the captivating and transforming truths of the last things. This book presents conference messages that so satisfyingly fed the souls of those in attendance.

The first part of this book provides scriptural studies on the last things. It begins with Michael Barrett's stirring message on the Day of the Lord from Zephaniah 1–2, in which, after depicting the terror and imminence of that Day, he calls us to flee not *from* the Judge, but *toward* the Judge, for He extends mercy to repentant sinners. This is followed by two messages from David Strain, the first one explaining what John's vision of the number of the sealed in Revelation 7 teaches us about the unspeakable joy that awaits us in Emmanuel's land. Strain's second message, on the last battle in Revelation 19:11–20:15, helps us see our daily life in the world with new eyes, as the arena of Christ's final victory. Finally, Daniel Timmer's incisive message on John's use of Isaiah in Revelation 21–22 gives us a sense of the beauty and glory of the new creation while providing clear biblical-theological principles to help us appreciate the striking unity between the Testaments.

Three topical studies comprise the second part of this book, the first being David Murray's practical look at the characteristics of the signs of the times, the perils of misinterpreting them, and what they mean for us today. Derek Thomas provides the next two messages. In the first, he describes the heaven that awaits us and that we hope for, and in the second, he outlines the biblical teaching on hell, especially from the lips of Jesus, while providing arguments against annihilationism.

The third part of the book gives us three historical studies. First, Greg Salazar's fascinating paper argues that the Puritans framed the eschatological statements of the Westminster Standards with a conscientious conservatism that enabled generations of believers who held differing millennial views to maintain unity. Let us follow the humble charity and unity modeled by the Puritans of the Westminster Assembly. Then, Adrian Neele gives us an inspiring analysis of the thoughts, journals, and sermons of Jonathan Edwards, revealing that, for Edwards, the themes of the beauty and glory of God, the Christian life, and the last things were a common and constant ever-developing thread of devotion. Thirdly, William VanDoodewaard's address on Thomas Boston shows us how a seasoned shepherd, through his sermons and journal entries, prepared both himself and his congregation for the appointment that no one can miss, by reminding himself, and us, of the interest we have in the covenant of grace through Christ.

In part four of this book we have two experiential studies. First, Joel Beeke gives us a panorama of the beauty and glory of the marriage supper of the lamb in Revelation 19:7–9, revealing that Christ, who makes heaven heavenly, is the one to whom we may one day be married in the greatest wedding of all time. May Christ, the centerpiece of heaven, be the centerpiece of our hearts! Finally, Gerald Bilkes's message on 1 Corinthians 15 gives us a taste and an expectation of the final victory, when the last Adam at the last trumpet defeats the last enemy. How wonderful and encouraging it is to have our hearts filled with the promise of Christ's victory and of the glory that awaits!

SCRIPTURAL STUDIES

CHAPTER 1

The Day of the Lord: Escaping the Inescapable (Zephaniah 1–2)

Michael P. V. Barrett

There are some texts in the Bible that leave us with happy consideration. There are some texts that the poorest of preachers can expound and transport hearers into the heavenly places. The great gospel themes of salvation deserve the attention of faithful preaching. But there is another side of the gospel that is never easy to preach and is often unpopular to pulpit and pew alike. But it is a vital message that highlights and intensifies the beauty of saving grace. God's sovereign love for sinners is understood to be all the more gracious in the light of His just wrath and judgment of sinners. It is on this hard word of judgment that I want to focus our thoughts in this address. We must understand that the way and end of transgressors is hard. Those outside of Christ must heed the warning of certain doom and flee to Christ. Those who know the safe refuge of grace must be ever grateful and increasingly diligent to see others enter the stronghold of grace and flee the wrath to come.

Our text is from Zephaniah—not a household name among the prophets, but one whose recorded pedigree is traced back to the good king Hezekiah. He preached during the reign of Josiah, king of Judah (Zeph. 1:1), in an era of corruption. After the forgotten reforms of Hezekiah, Zephaniah most likely helped to foster the yet to come reforms of Josiah. Zephaniah's ministry most likely did not cover the entire span of Josiah's lengthy reign from 640–609 BC, which is evident, for instance, from the fact that Nineveh's fall in 612 BC had not yet occurred (2:13). In addition, many of the sins cited in 1:3–13 were common before, but not after, Josiah's reforms. Second Chronicles 34:3–35:19 indicates that Josiah's reforms occurred in two stages: the first, in his 12th year, and the second, in his 18th year (that is, 628 and 622/621 BC). So, Zephaniah's preaching would have spanned between 640–621 BC, during the first half of Josiah's administration, making him contemporary with the early days of Jeremiah.[1]

Politically, socially, and spiritually, the nation tottered on the brink of collapse. To this depraved and perverted society, God raised up this prophet and gave him the authority of heaven (Zeph. 1:1) to warn sinners of the judgment to come. As a messenger of judgment, he announced the terrors of the Lord. He declared impending doom, called sinners to repentance, and unfolded the mercy of God. Zephaniah preached the whole counsel of God, a message of judgment and salvation.

As common for the prophets of his day, some aspects of his message saw near fulfillment in the Babylonian captivity, while other predictions leap forward to that ultimate divine judgment yet to come. It was a hard word to hear—a message of bad news about the terrors of the Lord to be let loose on the impenitent. But the announcement of bad news opened the very way for a call to repentance and for the unfolding of the mercy of God, the good news. The certain judgment of sinners is the reason for repentance. Whether we consider God's past or future work of judgment, there are lessons that are timeless and warnings that are universal. The God of the past or future is the same God of the present. Indeed, Zephaniah's message of judgment and grace assures us that God controls all of history and will vindicate His name in the final victory over sin and the ultimate salvation of His people. So, in this address, I want to consider Zephaniah's timelessly relevant message on how to escape the inescapable.

Divine Judgment is Just

God's judgment of sinners is never capricious; it is always earned and deserved. Nothing is quite as fearful as getting from God's hand what is deserved. Zephaniah gives two reasons for this fearful thought of God's judgment.

First, God's judgment is fearful because of who the Lord is. He is righteous. Zephaniah 3:5 refers to Him as the "just LORD," that is, the righteous Lord. The root word for "righteous" or "righteousness" designates

---

1. See this and other introductory notes of mine on Zephaniah in Joel R. Beeke et al., *The Reformation Heritage KJV Study Bible.* (Grand Rapids: Reformation Heritage Books, 2014).

straightness, and by extension, conformity to a standard of evaluation. It is not necessarily a moral term. For instance, a "path of righteousness" describes a straight path, one that does not curve or bend; or a "righteous balance" describes accuracy with regard to the standards for weights. But when the standard of evaluation is God's law, righteousness refers to moral conformity to that law. When it refers to God, it means that God conforms to Himself; God cannot deviate from who He is. That God is righteous simply means that God can be nothing other than what He is. As the psalmist declared, "the righteous LORD loveth righteousness" (11:7). This straightness, or conformity to the divine self-standard, extends to the entirety of His person and perfections, one of which is His infinite, eternal, and unchanging justice. Because God is inflexibly just as is evident in His person and expressed in His law, He cannot ignore or tolerate sin, which is totally contrary to His character. For sin to go unpunished would require God to waiver from Himself. His justice means that judging sin is the right thing for Him to do. Judgment is inescapable.

Second, God's judgment is fearful because of who sinners are. Verse 1:17 sums up the cause of the justly deserved judgment: "because they have sinned against the LORD." The word "sinned" is from a root meaning to miss a target, vividly picturing the sinner's missing the mark of God's perfect standard. This is no trivial matter, highlighted by Paul with his all-inclusive assessment that "all have sinned and come short" of God's glory. Remember that God is righteous and cannot tolerate the slightest deviation from His holy law. Significantly, Paul's conclusion in Romans 3:23 follows a detailed exposé of specific sins. Similarly, Zephaniah, anticipating the Pauline logic, exposes the people's sins with overwhelming and condemning evidence.

The people were *idolaters* (Zeph. 1:4, 5). They were guilty of breaking the first and greatest commandment. God requires total devotion (Deut. 6:5) and prohibits having any other god before Him (Ex. 20: 3). They did not love the Lord, but replaced Him with gods of their imagination and of the world around them. Their worship was a hellish mixture of Baal worship (a perverse fertility cult), astrology and magic (the host of heaven) with the professed worship of the one true God. They swore (pledged their allegiance) to both the LORD and to Malcham (a common designation of Baal). What a clear case of missing the mark of the first commandment as the people brought these "other gods before" the Lord! Tragically, they followed their religious leaders into these transgressions. There were renegade, black-robed priests of foreign gods, called the Chemarim, who seemed to work alongside the Levitical priests (the supposed legitimate clergy) in leading the people in this worship of nature and fate mixed with a bit of orthodoxy. They were attempting to cover all the bases, appealing to whatever god would do them good. Religion was a way of manipulating some god to satisfy personal needs—a religion for profit.

The manifestations of idolatry may look different today than they did then, although there are striking similarities with earth worshipers and cults led by charismatic leaders who use and abuse the Bible for personal gain. But whenever and however God is reduced to being nothing more than an instrument to be manipulated for personal satisfaction, His law is violated and those who are guilty are in jeopardy of judgment (especially in violation of the third commandment, Ex. 20:7). God demands love and total allegiance. He will not share His glory with another. Violating those demands is warrant for judgment.

The people were also spiritually *insensitive*: they "turned back from the LORD; and…have not sought the LORD, nor enquired for him" (Zech. 1:6). They recoiled from the Lord, drawing back and shrinking away from Him. Not seeking the Lord equates to spiritual ignorance (see Ps. 14:2). Without spiritual perception, they were alienated in their minds, insensitive to gospel grace, and doomed in their ignorance. This ignorance or insensitivity is no excuse; rather, it is another reason for God's just judgment. To have no bent toward God is to be bent toward hell. To have no heart for the Lord is certain doom. That was true then; it is true now.

The final piece of evidence proving their sin is that they were *incredulous* (Zech. 1:12). Those on the verge of judgment had no excuse for being ignorant because God had given them His word of warning. Throughout Israel's history, God had revealed Himself and His law; His expectations and demands were clear. Perhaps preaching to these same people, Jeremiah had said that the Lord had sent His servants the prophets "daily rising up early [an idiom expressing earnestness] and sending them: Yet they hearkened not unto me, nor inclined their ear, but hardened their heart" (Jer. 7:25–26). Likewise, Zephaniah addressed those who refused to believe the word of God. He refers to God's thorough searching as with a light to expose and punish those "that are settled on their lees: that say in their heart, The LORD will not do good, neither will he do evil" (1:12). The picture is of wine that has not been drained from its dregs and has thickened into a viscid sludge. The image describes those who are confirmed and hardened in their obstinate denial of God, His Word and His work. They interpreted the delay of what the prophets had warned as evidence that God was inactive and incapable. Peter encountered skepticism in his day regarding the same issue (2 Peter 3:4–15). There is something about the status quo that lulls unbelievers into complacency and denial of impending doom. But unbelief is a deadly sin that damns the soul.

The evidence is overwhelming. Sinners are justly under the wrath and condemnation of the righteously just and holy God. Zephaniah is a pattern for modern preachers to be bold in exposing sin and faithful in proclaiming the righteousness of God that includes His just wrath "against all ungodliness and unrighteousness of men" (Rom. 1:18). Part of gospel preaching is warning sinners of impending and inescapable judgment.

Divine Judgment is Terrible

It is a "fearful thing to fall into the hands of the living God" (Heb. 10:11) who is described as a "consuming fire" (Heb. 12:29) and just in all His ways. Zephaniah highlights three reasons why divine judgment is so terrible.

First, it is terrible *because of its source*. The judgment is divine. The prophet designates this judgment as the Day of the Lord (Zeph. 1:7, 14). This is why this text is fitting for a conference on the last days. The Day of the Lord became a frequent theme in prophetic preaching. This expression occurs around twenty times in the Old Testament, with fifty more corresponding designations occurring (a day belonging to the Lord, a day belonging to the Lord of Hosts, a day of vengeance belonging to the Lord, a day which is coming of the Lord, or simply, that day). Significantly, some of the most detailed expositions of the Day of the Lord appear in the earliest of the writing prophets (Obadiah and Joel in the 9th century BC, on my dating of these books), and are carried throughout both the Major and Minor Prophets. Zephaniah's description and development of the Day is one of the most explicit.

The Day of the Lord refers to God's spectacular intervention in time to bring retribution against wickedness and deliverance for righteousness. The Day of the Lord is when eternity breaks into time. It does not refer to a 24-hour period, but rather to an indefinite time when God interrupts human history in an extraordinary way, either for judgment or blessing. It may be a good day or a bad day, depending on one's relationship with the Lord: the same day can be a dread for sinners but a delight for saints. Indeed, there are components of this day that include punishment, salvation, and the blessings associated with the Messiah and His kingdom. It is true that God providentially governs the events and circumstances of time. Providence is His ordinary work. The Day of the Lord, on the other hand, is His extraordinary and unique work. This extraordinary and unique work can be accomplished with or without the use of secondary means (like natural disasters or foreign armies). But even when secondary means are employed, it is clear that they are just instruments in God's hand to accomplish His special purpose. For instance, locust plagues happened in regular cycles, but there was something about the locusts in Joel's day that he recognized as extraordinary: "Alas for the day! for the day of the LORD is at hand, and as a destruction from the Almighty shall it come" (Joel 1:15). And that was just a precursor of a more devastating day that was imminent, terrible, and irresistible (Joel 2).

It is important to understand that there have been multiple days of the Lord, all of which are types, or picture prophecies, of the final, eschatological Day that is yet to come. For instance, the Day of the Lord against Edom (Obadiah) and Babylon (Isaiah 14) are matters of ancient history, but those past days point to the appointed day when God "will judge the world in righteousness" (Acts 17:30). On the one hand, some components of Zephaniah's announcement of the coming Day of the Lord found fulfillment in Babylon's destruction of Jerusalem (which, though it is past, still illustrates timeless and universal principles). On the other hand, some components of Zephaniah's prophecy refer specifically to the eschaton and have yet to be fulfilled. Prophets often juxtaposed near prophecies with distant prophecies, telescoping the events without reference to time intervals that separated the events.

The extraordinary divine activity of the Day of the Lord is underscored by the verbs expressing the divine initiative. Consider Zephaniah 1:2–4, 7–9, 12, 17. The prerogative and execution of judgment belong to God. It is thus not surprising that Nahum asked, "Who can stand before his indignation? And who can abide in the fierceness of his anger?" (Nah. 1:6). The psalmist's answer to this question is likewise not surprising, "the ungodly shall not stand in the judgment" (Ps. 1:5). There is no contest, no appeal, no excuse, no escape. Joel describes the inescapable terrors of this day: "Multitudes, multitudes in the valley of decision: for the day of the LORD is near in the valley of decision" (Joel 3:14). The thought here is not that those in the valley have the opportunity to decide their own fate; on the contrary, they are in the valley of that which has been divinely decreed. They have no hope; they have no way of escape. Amos illustrates this imminence in almost tragic comedy when he compares trying to escape the Day of Lord with a man who flees from a lion to the supposed safety of his home, only to encounter a bear and be bitten by a serpent (Amos 5:19).

Zephaniah, in a most startling expression, puts in bold the divine source of the judgment when he equates the Day of the Lord with the Lord's sacrifice that He has prepared, or more literally, consecrated (1:7–8). The sacrifice speaks of satisfaction. Justice must be satisfied. What a statement this is, testifying to God's inflexible justice that must be appeased! That satisfaction will be made either by the sinner himself in eternal damnation or by Jesus who satisfied God's infinite justice by His self-sacrifice for His people. The message of judgment is therefore an occasion for the message of grace, which we will see shortly.

Next, the judgment is terrible *because of its horrors* (1:15–17). In verses 15 and 16, Zephaniah describes "that day" six different ways, linking the word "day" with some dreadful characteristic. It seems to parallel the six days of creation, when God made everything good, with six devastations of creation's reversal, making everything bad.

1) It will be a day of "wrath," referring to God's rage and fury—His passionate yet controlled outbursts of anger. Significantly, Peter describes the final Day in terms of a

fire that will engulf the heavens and the earth (2 Peter 3:7, 10, 12). It is as though the heat of God's anger kindles the flames of destruction.

2) It will be "a day of trouble and distress," referring to the effects of God's outpoured wrath. From every side, sinners caught in this judgment will feel pressure and suffocation as they are choked by the fumes of God's anger in the flames of hell.

3) It will be "a day of wasteness and desolation," referring to the utter ruin and emptiness of catastrophe.

4) It will be "a day of darkness and gloominess," without a ray of hope and with all the fears and anxiety associated with the dark.

5) It will be "a day of clouds and thick darkness," suggestive of the clouds engulfing Sinai at the giving of the law, which is the righteous standard that sentences the guilty to this terrible day.

6) It is "a day of the trumpet and alarm." The trumpet or ram's horn was the instrument used in the course of battle, either to warn of the approaching enemy or to signal a force's advance or retreat. Here, it sounds the alarm of danger, but it is too late to retreat. The battle has been lost; escape is impossible.

Verse 17 vividly sums up the horrors of this judgment: "I will bring distress upon men, that they shall walk like blind men...and their blood shall be poured out as dust, and their flesh as the dung." "Bringing distress" conveys the idea of harassing or pressing hard against another with hostility. Zephaniah's description of the objects of God's hostility, as those walking like blind men, parallels Isaiah's image of sinners as those walking in darkness, groping for the wall like the blind, and stumbling at noon as in the night (Isa. 59:9–10). It is a picture of total hopelessness. That their blood is as dust and their flesh as dung indicates the worthlessness of life. The point of the comparison is not so much the quantity of what is poured out like dust, but the quality. Blood, and by metonymy, the life it represents, is as worthless as the dirt under foot. Their flesh is like dung.

The most careful exegesis cannot escape the fact that dung is dung. It is not a pretty statement, but rather a vivid picture of that which is despised. If the "six days" of verses 15 and 16 allude to a reversal of creation, verse 17 is the climax of that analogy. In the original creation at the apex of the creation week, man was made in the image of God. But sin has corrupted and marred that image. In the final judgment, that which enjoyed honor in time is forever dishonored in death. The description of judgment is terrible. How much more terrible will be the reality!

Finally, the judgment is terrible *because of its certainty*: "The great day of the LORD is near, it is near, and hasteth greatly" (1:14; compare verse 7 where "at hand" is the same as the word "near"). The language expresses both certainty and imminence. This is no idle threat; indeed, it is just about to happen. This teaches us something important about the predictive words of Scripture. Predictive prophecy tends to use the language of imminence. This means that regardless of how distant the prophecy is from its actual fulfillment, the prediction is made as though its fulfillment were impending. This intentional temporal ambiguity is one of the most significant features of prophetic language. Since the time of fulfillment is not specified, the application of the prophecy is not limited. To attempt to precisely date a prophecy would effectively rob it of its purpose to affect the hearts of those living in the pre-fulfillment generations.

Because of common misunderstandings of how prophecy works, let us reiterate an important point. In one sense, the fulfillment of this Day of the Lord prophecy against Jerusalem was intended for that specific generation. In another sense, this prophecy, like each of the multiple Day of the Lord prophecies throughout the prophetic corpus, projects an eschatological day that will signal the end of time as we know it. This does not mean that a single prophecy is fulfilled over and again. Rather, each prophecy finds a single, ultimate fulfillment. Nevertheless, even the past "Days" typify the final eschatological day. Every judgment of the ungodly parallels and points to what God will do on that final day.

My point of application is this: Just as it is certain that Jerusalem's destruction occurred in the 6th century BC, so with the same certainty will the climactic day of the Lord occur when God has determined. Do not misinterpret the longsuffering of God that delays its execution to be evidence of divine inactivity. Heed the warnings now while there is time and opportunity so that when the Day comes you may be "found of him in peace, without spot, and blameless" (2 Peter 3:14). Otherwise, the judgment will be inescapable.

Divine Judgment is Discriminating

Zephaniah shines forth a glimmer of hope in what is mostly a hopeless message. Two thoughts set the tension.

First, judgment is *inescapable for unrepentant sinners*. This is true because of its extent. God's ultimate judgment is universal. Zephaniah 1:2–3 reveal that no part of the world is exempt. The prophet depicts a destruction of man and beast that is as wide and sweeping as the flood that destroyed the world in the days of Noah. Note Peter's link between the flood and the fire of judgment (2 Peter 3:5–7). There will be no place to hide in that day (see Amos 5; Rev. 6). The judgment is also particular in that it extends to every class of man, from royalty to servants (1:8–9). This contrast is an example of mer-ismus, a literary device that uses two opposite parts of a thing to designate a whole. Referring to the extremes of royalty and servants, all classes of humanity in between are affected. God is no respecter of persons—not in salvation, not in judgment.

This judgment is also inescapable because of the futility of human efforts. Verse 17 pictured the helplessness of sinners who walk around as blind men groping and grabbing what they can but to no avail. Verse 18 describes absolute human inability: "Neither their silver nor their gold shall be able to deliver them in the day of the LORD's wrath." All buying power is deflated; people cannot buy or bribe their way out of judgment. Psalm 49 makes it clear that self-redemption is impossible because the cost of a soul is more expensive than any can afford; every attempt is futile (49:8). This is why Peter says we are not redeemed with corruptible things like silver and gold (1 Peter 1:18). Man has no currency recognized by God. Self-salvation is impossible.

Second, judgment is *escapable to repentant sinners*. There is a message of hope after all. There is a way to escape judgment that is contrary to human reasoning. At the sight of danger, common sense says to flee the potential destruction: go as far and as fast as possible in the opposite direction. But when the danger is divine wrath, faith demands that we run to the Source of the destruction, for mercy.

Zephaniah gives the invitation to those under the sentence of destruction: "Gather yourselves together, yea gather together, O nation not desired" (2:1) and then "Seek ye the LORD, all the meek of the earth" (2:3). The invitations are instructive. The word "gather" comes from a root meaning "to pick up stubble." It pictures one who is stooping down; it is a picture of humiliation. The expression "not desired" literally has the idea of turning pale, depicting the shame resulting from the consciousness of sin. It is an image showing the contrition and confession that are such essential components of repentance. Seeking the Lord is a form of the verb (*piel*) that functions as an iterative, a repeated and habitual seeking. The meek are not those who are humble as an innate character trait, but rather as those who are poor and needy, helpless in themselves, and without any resources to care for themselves. To so seek the Lord is to find Him, for He promises to allow Himself to be found by those who seek Him with all of their heart: "if ye seek him, he will be found of you" (2 Chron. 15:2; note the tolerative sense from the *niphal* stem). Rather than trying to outrun judgment, we must run to the Judge as the only hope. It is those who acknowledge that they are helpless who find help in Him.

Zephaniah offers the hope of safety for those who repent: "it may be ye shall be hid in the day of the LORD's anger" (2:3). This is not an expression of doubt but of hope. It is not presumption but faith that God will be found by those who seek Him. The unbreakable promise is that those who come unto Him He will in no wise cast out (John 6:37).

But the prophet, as a preacher of the gospel, presses the urgency of this invitation to repent. Zephaniah 2:2 iterates the urgency: "Before the decree bring forth, before the day pass as the chaff, before the fierce anger of the LORD come upon you, before the day of the LORD's anger come upon you." Once the Day of the Lord comes it will be too late: escaping will be impossible. Do not find yourself in the valley of decision; flee to God against the coming day. And the day is coming; like the chaff blowing in the wind, the day is rushing ever near. It is both foolish and impossible to speculate or set dates for the coming of the Day of the Lord. But one thing is absolutely certain: It is nearer today than it has ever been before. Today is the day of salvation; tomorrow is the day of destruction. Be certain that justice will be served—either in self forever or in Christ.

The paths to eternity may differ for us—for one, it is death, and for another, it is Christ's return—but the destination is the same. Outside of Christ, there is nothing "but a certain fearful looking for of judgment and fiery indignation" (Heb. 10:27)—and no escape. In Christ, we have the hope of glory (Col. 1:27). The only way to escape the inescapable is through Jesus: the only way, truth, and life.

CHAPTER 2

The Number of the Sealed
(Revelation 7)

David Strain

The subject of the last things, which is our special focus during this conference, is at once enormously intriguing—full of fascination for the Christian public—and immensely perplexing—full of interpretive enigmas for the Christian preacher. This means that, while your interest levels are likely to be quite high as you read, my confidence levels are to be very low as I attempt to explain! Nevertheless, let us consider Revelation 7, a chapter that I believe ought to hold peculiar comfort and encouragement for us in our particular cultural moment.

Let us first consider the context for the vision now before us. In chapters 5 and 6, the prophet John sees a vision of the exalted Christ, the victorious Lamb, opening a scroll with seven seals. The scroll is the great symbol of the plan of God for the unfolding of history between the first and final coming of Jesus Christ. When no one was found to open the scroll, John was overcome with grief. It looked to him as if the wickedness of the world would prevail and the purposes of God would fail—until, that is, an elder came to him, doing what good elders should. He preached Christ to John: "Weep not!" he said. "The Lion of the tribe of Judah, the Root of David, hath prevailed to open the book, and to loose the seven seals thereof" (Rev. 5:2). Jesus the Conqueror holds the scroll of the divine decree in His hand, and He brings the plan of the Father to pass.

And so John wipes away his tears and turns to look for this mighty Lion, and in the middle of the throne he sees a Lamb instead, standing as though it had been slain—His "wounds, yet visible above, in beauty glorified." And in chapter 6 he begins to open the scroll, and with each seal that Christ opens, a different facet of life between the two comings of our Savior is revealed. The first four seals speak of various afflictions poured out upon the world as warnings of the final judgment to come. The fifth seal focuses on the fact of the sufferings through which the church in particular must pass during this period until Jesus returns. The sixth seal gives us a glimpse of that final cataclysm, so terrible that those who experience it cry out for the mountains and rocks to fall on them and hide them from the face of the Lord on the throne, and from the wrath of the Lamb: "For the great day of his wrath is come; and who shall be able to stand?" (Rev. 6:17).

Actually, that question is a crucial one, and many of us, even in the church, find ourselves asking it. The world isn't asking it. They will, John says, but only at the end, when it's too late. But those of us who follow Jesus find ourselves asking it now. Who can stand? In a day when the pressure to capitulate to the new sexual ethics of the LGBTQI+ paradigm is enormous, who can stand? When wickedness is normalized—even celebrated—on TV screens and by officials in high office, who stand? In a day like ours when to follow Jesus can be costly, fraught with social stigma, and even legal sanction, there are times when we are overwhelmed. And we begin to wonder if we're going to make it. And we find ourselves asking, "Who can stand?"

Revelation 7 is something of an interlude between the sixth and seventh seal in the scroll. And it is designed to answer that question for hurting fearful Christians. It presents two scenes, two related images of the church, the aim of each is to comfort and encourage us in the midst of the trials we endure.

Today's Tribulation

When the tectonic plates that make up the earth's crust collide, the enormous pressures involved can result in earthquakes and volcanic eruptions. We've all seen the recent images of Hawaiian lava flows engulfing trees and cars and homes. That kind of tectonic collision, with the terrifying effects it can produce, I think, is a helpful illustration of the way John pictures the clash of the kingdom of God with the rebel kingdom of this world in the book of Revelation. With the life, death, and resurrection of Jesus Christ, the kingdom of God erupted onto the scene of history, and ever since a tectonic collision has been the result. In verse 13 of the chapter before us, John asks one of the elders about the identity of the vast company in white robes that he sees. And he is told that: "These are they which came out of great tribulation, and have washed their robes, and made them white in the blood of the Lamb."

The word he uses here, "tribulation" (*thlipsis* in Greek), evokes the kind of tectonic collision we've been describing. It carries the idea of pressure, of conflict, and of terrible weight, bearing down upon us, threatening to crush us. John sees a vision of those who come out of this great tribulation. And note carefully the present tense of the participle: "These are the ones coming out—*already, right now, at the time of writing*; they are coming out of the *thlipsis*, the tectonic collision of two kingdoms—the kingdom of Christ, and the kingdom of the rebel world."

So, "the great tribulation," whatever our dispensational friends might say, doesn't refer to some short time of intense persecution in the final few years of history, just before Jesus comes back. Rather, it's a way to speak about the experience of the whole church during all the long years between Christ's comings. This is life while His kingdom presses into the world and the world violently reacts to His kingdom. It's *thlipsis*—the great tribulation! That's life, here and now, isn't it? We can see abundant evidence of this clash all around us. Read a newspaper. What do you see? *Thlipsis*—the church under attack, the world in revolt!

I start here because it's important to understand that one use of biblical eschatology (the study of the last things) isn't to feed our curiosity or fuel conspiracy theories as we try, for instance, to fit our understanding of end time events into the daily news. No, the main use of biblical eschatology is to help us face the real world; to understand life here and now, without leading us either to triumphalism or despair. "Beloved, think it not strange concerning the fiery trial which is to test you, as though some strange thing happened unto you" (1 Peter 4:12). This is normal. So get ready! Jesus made the same point in John 16:33: "In this world you shall have tribulation," He said. Or think of Paul warning the church in Acts 14:22: "We must through much tribulation enter into the kingdom of God." What's the take-away here? "Get your expectations right! This is the normal Christian life. This is life here, while the kingdom of God collides with a rebel world. It's *thlipsis*—the great tribulation!"

That dose of realism helps us face the challenges before us and train our children to do the same with courage and humility and determination to suffer for Christ's sake. But along with that sobering realism, there is wonderful encouragement here, and that's what Revelation 7 is really all about. Scan over it and you will quickly see that there are two scenes; the first in verses 1–8, and the second in verses 9–17. The first, we might say, focuses our attention on the church's security, while the second highlights the church's celebration. And we're going to look at each in turn.

The Church's Security (vv. 1–8)

John sees four angels holding back four winds. Verses 2 and 3 explain that they have the power to harm the earth and the sea, but a fifth angel tells them to hold back the wind, "till we have sealed the servants of our God in their foreheads" (v. 3). Now, what is this image of a seal on the forehead designed to teach us? There are two pieces of biblical data that I think offer some help.

Secured by Name
The first comes from a parallel passage in Revelation 14:1, where John says, "And I looked, and, lo, a Lamb stood on the mount Sion, and with him an hundred forty and four thousand." John sees the Lamb and the 144,000 observes that they "had his name and his Father's name written in their foreheads." John is connecting this vision to the one in Revelation 7 so that the seal of God that the angel is to place on the foreheads of the servants of our God (Revelation 7), is the same as the name of the Lamb and of the Father (Revelation 14).

I have a very dear member of my congregation in Jackson, Mississippi who has a running joke with her adult children about how they've already claimed their favorite pieces of furniture and ornaments in her home, so that when she dies, if you look underneath any given ornament you'll find a sticker with the name of one of her children on it. They've put their name on the furniture and claimed it beyond all dispute. John's vision is telling us that God has put His name upon His people and claimed them for Himself once and for all. He has sealed His people with His name; they belong to Him, and nothing can snatch them out of His hands.

Secured by the Spirit

The second set of biblical data comes from the Apostle Paul. In Ephesians 1:13 he says that Christians are "sealed with that holy Spirit of promise." Notice this carefully. The Holy Spirit *Himself* is the seal. In Ephesians 4:30 we are exhorted not to grieve the Holy Spirit by whom we "are sealed unto the day of redemption." There is a future orientation to this sealing of the Spirit: for the day of redemption. In 2 Corinthians 1:22, Paul even says that God sealed us and gave us "the earnest of the Spirit in our hearts." The Spirit is the one by whom the Father and the Son put Their name on us, and claims us as Their own. Our future is guaranteed by God. He Himself is the guarantee, the deposit, and the down-payment of an unfading inheritance yet to come.

There's a marvelous Trinitarianism in the biblical teaching on this point. The Spirit is the seal, by whom the name of the Lamb, and of His Father, are placed upon us. We have fellowship with all three persons of the Blessed Trinity. And in that fellowship, John says, there is a preservation and security. As Jesus prayed in John 17, "I have manifested thy name unto them.... Holy Father...keep them in thy name." To be sealed is to have the Spirit imprint upon us the name, to introduce us into fellowship with the Father and with His Son Jesus Christ. It is to be claimed by God as God's own, preserved, kept in His name. The lesson of Revelation 7 is not that the blasting winds of tribulation will not blow. It is that the servants of God are sealed, so that when the winds blow, God's servants are kept. They are not swept away. They are secure.

There's a great story told of A. W. Pink during his days on the Isle of Lewis, in the highlands of Scotland. Pink, as you may know, was a famously cantankerous man. And every day he would march down to the harbor to buy fresh fish for his supper. On one occasion he was recognized. Now, in Scotland, when people inquire about your health, quite often they will ask, "How are you keeping?" So, "How are you keeping today, Mr. Pink?" a man asked. Without breaking his stride or missing a beat, Pink replied, as only Pink could, "Not keeping! Being kept!" Isn't that the message here? Not keeping! Being kept!

What good news for a suffering church! What a relief for a world-weary Christian! We are being kept! We have been sealed. We are the bearers of the divine name. We have been introduced into fellowship with the triune God, in union with Jesus Christ, and by the work of the Holy Spirit. And nothing can ever shatter that bond. Nothing can fracture that union. Peter says that we are "kept by the power of God through faith unto salvation ready to be revealed in the last time" (1 Peter 1:5)! Or as Paul put it so wonderfully, "Neither death, nor life, nor angels, nor principalities, nor powers, nor things present, nor things to come, nor height, nor depth, nor any other creature, shall be able to separate us from the love of God, which is in Christ Jesus our Lord" (Rom. 8:38–39). Praise God for the glorious security that belongs to His servants!

Secured to the Last Man

But who are these servants of God who are sealed? Verse 4 says, "And I heard the number of them which were sealed: and there were sealed an hundred and forty and four thousand of all the tribes of the children of Israel." Now, John isn't teaching that only 144,000 Jewish people enjoy this marvelous protection during these days of tribulation and trial. The number 144,000 is, as one scholar puts it, "a suspiciously tidy sort of number that is much more likely to be a symbol than a statistic."[1] If you multiply the number of the tribes of Israel (12) by itself (12 x 12), and if the whole is multiplied by a thousand (144 x 1,000), you make an emphatic point without ambiguity that this is the full number of the whole people of God. We also know that John isn't thinking literally about the people of God if we consider the way he lists the tribes, from each of whom 12,000 are drawn. First, there is no precedence in Scripture for the order in which John lists them. Reuben is usually first, but here it's the tribe of Judah. Judah is the royal tribe from which the Lord Jesus came, the Lion of the Tribe of Judah, the Root of David, as the elder in Revelation 5 put it. And now that He has come, the people of God are made new. That's why John omits the tribe of Dan and puts in Manasseh. John is tinkering with the list of the twelve tribes, something no devout Jewish man would ever dare do, in order to make a theological point—that Jesus reconfigures the Israel of God. For, as the elders sing in Revelation 5:9–10, "Thou art worthy...for thou wast slain, and hast redeemed us to God by thy blood out of every

---

1. Darrell W. Johnson, *Discipleship on the Edge: An Expository Journey Through The Book of Revelation*, (Vancouver, B.C.: Regent College Publishing, 2004),183.

kindred, and tongue, and people, and nation; and hast made us unto our God kings and priests: and we shall reign on the earth."

Who gets a seal? Who gets the preserving-keeping-guarding-protecting Spirit of God, guaranteeing our inheritance? Who gets the divine name? Who is entered into fellowship with the Father, in the Son, by the Spirit? Who is it that will be guarded by the power of God unto salvation ready to be revealed in the last time? Every single believer in Jesus Christ, without a single one left out! Not one is missing! The weakest believer, the most fearful, the youngest in the faith, those who struggle and stumble and often fall, those who cling to Jesus but fear their grip of Him isn't strong enough—every child of God, every one on them is sealed by the promised Holy Spirit:

> The soul that on Jesus hath leaned for repose
> I will not, I will not desert to his foes.
> That soul, though all hell should endeavor to shake,
> I'll never, no never, no never forsake![2]

That is His promise to you, in the great tribulation, in the thick of the seismic conflict between the kingdom of Christ and the world that hates Him. "I'll never let you go! I have put My Spirit in you. You have union with Christ. I've put My name upon you. And I'll never, no never, no never forsake you!"

The Church's Celebration (vv. 9–17)

In verses 1–8, John hears about the number of the sealed. But in verse 9, he turns to look at them: they are a great multitude that no one could number of all nations, tribes, peoples, and tongues. Not just Jewish believers, but Barbarians, Scythians, slaves and free…Michiganders and Mississippians…and even a few Scots too! Everyone who was sealed now celebrates. This is the same church described in verse 4 as the 144,000 enduring the great trial of life amidst tribulation, only now he views them having finished the race, now gathered in great victory. John sees the same group in verses 9–17 that he saw in verses 1–8, but now at a different stage. In verses 1–8, he sees the church militant, but in 9–17 it's the church triumphant. Again, in verses 1–8 it's the church suffering, but in 9–17 it's the church

---

2. The Trinity Hymnal, *How Firm A Foundation*, (Suwanee, Ga.: Great Commission Publications, 1990), 94.

celebrating. And so here they are, in verse 9, standing "before the throne, and before the Lamb, clothed with white robes, and palms in their hands," crying out "with a loud voice, saying, Salvation to our God which sitteth upon the throne, and unto the Lamb." And as the church triumphant begins to sing, John says, the angels, and the elders, and the four living creatures—the whole heavenly court assembled before the Lord—take up the refrain. They join the celebration as heaven reverberates with anthems of praise: "Amen: Blessing, and glory, and wisdom, and thanksgiving, and honour, and power, and might, be unto our God for ever and ever. Amen."

Celebrating Grace Undeserved

What a celebration! But the congregation is not singing songs of self-congratulation, is it? "We made it! We made it! What a relief!" Rather, the wonder that will fuel endless praise down throughout eternity will be the clear realization of our own weakness, our own vulnerability to defection, how close we came to making shipwreck, time and time again, and yet at every turn the God who sits on the throne and the Lamb kept us, and preserved us. He pulled us back from the brink. He rescued us from the disaster our sin and stupidity would otherwise have brought.

If there *is* any room for any thought of self when we come into the presence of the exalted Christ at last, surely we will ask in amazement, "How ever did I come here? What a weak and foolish man I was! How inevitable my destruction seemed! How pathetic my flimsy resolutions! How fickle my best determination to follow Jesus! And yet, here I am, in the great congregation dressed, not in filthy rags, but in white robes, with a palm branch in my hand! What can account for it? There can be only one explanation: "Salvation to our God which sitteth upon the throne, and unto the Lamb!"

> I hear the Savior say,
> "Thy strength indeed is small;
> Child of weakness, watch and pray,
> Find in Me thine all in all."
>
> And when before the throne
> I stand in Him complete,
> I'll lay my trophies down,
> All down at Jesus' feet.

Jesus paid it all,
All to Him I owe;
Sin had left a crimson stain,
He washed it white as snow.[3]

It was Ed Clowney who said that the whole Bible can be summed up in one phrase: "Salvation belongs to the Lord." On the great day described in our text, we will come to know and rejoice in that truth like never before. "Salvation to our God which sitteth upon the throne, and unto the Lamb!"

Celebration Sustained: Qualification, Comfort, Communion
Now, as we close, look with me quickly at the fascinating conversation that takes place in verses 13–17. The interpreting elder explains three vital concluding truths. First he tells John about the qualifications, then he tells him about the comforts, and finally he tells him about the communion enjoyed by those who join the final celebration. We don't have time to do more than outline them here in brief.

First, consider the qualifications: who shall come there? On what basis do they gain entry? It turns out there is a dress code for heavenly glory. Verse 14, "These are they which came out of great tribulation, and have washed their robes, and made them white in the blood of the Lamb." The only people who take up the song, "Salvation to our God, and unto the Lamb," the only people who find a place in the final celebration are those whose robes have been washed white in the Lamb's blood.

I won't pretend to know your heart, dear friend. But it may be that you have filled your days with acts of religious devotion. You've devoted yourself to piety and to prayer. You've worked at the mastery of theological precision. You may have even stood in the pulpit and opened the scriptures to others. But when the final day comes, you can't point to any of these as a qualification. None of these will count for your entry into the great congregation. No, the gates of glory open only for those who meet the dress code. You must have white robes, washed in the blood of the Lamb. Jesus must wash you clean. Have you been washed, have you been washed in the blood

---

3. "Jesus Paid It All," *The Trinity Hymnal* (Suwanee, Ga.: Great Commission Publications, 1990), 308.

of the cross? Nothing else will qualify you for a place in that great joyful assembly.

Next, consider the comforts enjoyed by those who find a place in the final congregation. In place of the many sore trials of the great tribulation through which they have passed, the elder tells john in verse 16–17, "They shall hunger no more, neither thirst any more; neither shall the sun light on them, nor any heat. For the Lamb which is in the midst of the throne shall feed them, and shall lead them unto living fountains of waters: and God shall wipe away all tears from their eyes." Not hunger, not thirst, not sorrow—no, now the Lamb who washed us, He will shepherd us. The Lamb will be our shepherd. I suppose there is no better qualified shepherd than the one described as the Lamb. He knows what we need. He knows our frame and remembers that we are but dust, and He will lead us to green pastures and quiet waters to perfectly, endlessly, gloriously restore or souls.

The qualifications, comforts, and now, finally—and this surely is the blessing that makes heaven *heaven*—the elder tells John about the communion enjoyed by those who join the great congregation. Consider again verses 15–17: "Therefore are they before the throne of God, and serve him day and night in his temple: and he that sitteth on the throne shall dwell among them…the Lamb which is in the midst of the throne shall feed them, and shall lead them unto living fountains of waters."

The chief glory of heaven is fellowship with God in Jesus Christ—face to face at last with the Lamb. Rutherford was right: the Lamb is all the glory in Emmanuel's land! We will serve Him before the throne day and night. He will dwell among us. The Lamb will shepherd us, and so the living waters we only taste here, sustaining us through the desert places of this life, will completely satisfy our hearts hereafter. We will have Him. He will dwell with us in uninterrupted, unbreakable fellowship; no sin to obscure His face, no misunderstanding to cloud our communion. He will give Himself to us, and we will dwell in His presence forever. What a day that will be! No wonder they sing! Salvation to our God which sitteth upon the throne, and unto the Lamb!

May that day come quickly. Amen.

CHAPTER 3

The Last Battle
(Revelation 19:11–20:15)

David Strain

They spent thousands of dollars getting there in time for the winter migration, and countless hours waiting for a sighting. At last the whale watchers off the coast of Sydney, Australia finally caught a glimpse of one of the massive creatures. And soon every eye in the boat was glued to the starboard side, scanning the grey waters for another sign of the massive humpback whale that had briefly broken the surface just a few minutes before—which is why they missed it completely when the same whale, significantly longer and heavier than the boat the tourists were in, breached, in a massive leap, entirely out of the water, only two or three feet from the port side of their vessel! The boat behind them got a spectacular view of the whole event, but the folks in the lead boat missed it completely. They were all looking in the wrong direction.

We come to a passage in Revelation that, unless we are careful, will leave us looking out the starboard side of the boat while missing all the action happening on the port side. To put it bluntly, Christians are entirely too obsessed with the meaning of the 1,000 years spoken of in Revelation 20:1–6. We want to know if it's a literal thousand years. We want to know if it takes place before or after the return of Christ. And all the while our attention is fixed on the starboard side of the boat, we miss the big idea we're supposed to see on the port side.

Look at Revelation 19:11: "And I saw heaven opened, and behold a white horse; and he that sat upon him was called Faithful and True, and in righteousness he doth judge and make war." Here's the real focus of this part of the book. It's not the church. It's not the world or the devil. It's not even the meaning of the 1,000 years. The focus of our text, like the book of Revelation as a whole, is the person and work of Jesus Christ, the one who is called Faithful and True. This is, after all, "the revelation of Jesus Christ" (1:1). And so as we come to this important section of the book, let's resist the temptation to get distracted by points of controversy in the church at large, and instead strive together to keep our eyes trained on the Lord Jesus, whom our souls so badly need. What we have is two perspectives on the same event; as though two reporters had been dispatched to the front lines, and are sending back their reports to the newsroom. We get two complementary but distinct accounts of the same thing. Revelation 19:11–21 looks at the triumph of Christ, the warrior king, while Revelation 20:1–15 deals with the triumph of the church, Christ's warrior kingdom.

The Triumph of Christ, the Warrior King (Rev. 19:11–21)

The first six verses are entirely occupied with an extraordinary description of Jesus. John doesn't rush into a treatment of what Jesus is doing in our dark days. He doesn't focus too quickly on the unfolding plan of God playing out in history. No, he lingers first on the one sitting on the great white war horse—Jesus Christ, the triumphant warrior king. He dwells on each component of the vision, as though savoring each detail. For John, far more important than understanding what Christ is doing, is knowing Christ Himself. Everything flows from this. True comfort and consolation for a suffering church are rooted in this. There is nothing more important for us to do, no discipline more helpful for us to cultivate in these dark days than this. We must linger long with John on the person of Jesus Christ.

Look how He is described. Back in Revelation 1:5 Jesus was called "the faithful witness." Here He is called Faithful and True. That is to say, because He is faithful and true, He is a perfectly just judge—reliable, trustworthy; His eyes, Revelation 19:12, "were as a flame of fire." And again, this is just how John saw Jesus back in Revelation 1:14—eyes like flames of fire. Jesus sees, and His gaze penetrates. Nothing is hidden from His view, and He looks with perfect, blazing purity upon all who come before Him to be judged. And notice He wears "many crowns." In Revelation 12:3 and 13:1 both the great dragon, Satan himself, and the beast, the anti-Christian powers of the world, wear many crowns. But they are counterfeit kings, and their kingdom is set up in rivalry and rebellion. But Jesus is the true and only King of kings, and all the crowns of all the lands belong to Him as their rightful Lord. And recall how, back in chapter 4, verses 10–11, the twenty-four elders before God's throne cast their crowns before the throne and worship God, saying "Thou art worthy, O Lord, to receive glory and honour and power: for thou hast created all things, and for thy pleasure they are and were created." It was an image of believers surrendering themselves to the Lordship of God. Well, now here are those crowns, resting on the head of King Jesus. He wears your crown on His head! He is King, not only of all the nations, but in even the private realm of your life! And more than that, John says He has "a name that no man knows but he himself." That is to say, though He has shown us so much of Himself in Scripture, though we know Him truly, and may, by God's grace grow to know Him more and more profoundly, we will never know Him exhaustively. It will be, I believe, the greatest joy of every citizen of the new creation to spend eternity together discovering more and still more of the wonder of His great name, the mystery of His glorious person, and the beauty of His two natures. There are depths of mystery in Jesus Christ that only He can fathom. He has a name only He knows.

Then look at verse 13. It says He is clothed "with a vesture dipped in blood." I like what Darrell Johnson says at this point: "There is blood on his robe before he comes to the final battle." He continues,

> His robe is stained before he comes to the final battle. The question is, whose blood is it? From the whole of the book of Revelation, and from the whole of the New Testament, there is only one answer: the blood on the robe is his own. His robe, both a priest's robe and a king's robe, is stained with his own blood.[1]

The great truth we must never lose sight of is that Jesus Christ conquers and reigns, not because He will win a battle yet to be fought, but because He has already triumphed by the blood of the cross.

And He is called "The Word of God," John says. Recall that this was how John identified Him in the prologue of his gospel:

> In the beginning was the Word, and the Word was with God, and the Word was God. The same was in the beginning with God. All things were made by him; and without him was not

---

1. Darrell W. Johnson, *Discipleship on the Edge: An Expository Journey Through The Book of Revelation* (Vancouver, B.C.: Regent College Publishing, 2004), 327.

any thing made that was made…and the Word was made flesh
and dwelt among us (John 1:1–4).

That's Jesus Christ. That's who comes riding onto the battlefield of history: the Word who reveals God, who is God, who makes all things.
Waves are stilled when He speaks. Demons cower at His command.

No wonder "the armies which were in heaven followed him
upon white horses, clothed in fine linen, white and clean"! Who can
stand against Him? He is the mighty Word of God! And so, verse 15
says "out of his mouth goeth a sharp sword, that with it he should
smite the nations." The sword of His mouth, the word of the gospel,
conquers the world! There is no question about the success of the
gospel, is there? It's not in doubt.

Those of us in Christian ministry need to hear this word of
encouragement sometimes, don't we? After all, haven't there been
times when we've keenly felt our lack of success? Haven't we wor-
ried over our apparent failures? And isn't it easy in those moments
to begin to question if our confidence in the Word—in preaching
the Word, explaining the Word—hasn't been misplaced? Maybe the
Word needs supplementing, we wonder, and we begin to look for
gimmicks and shortcuts and marketing techniques to stay ahead
of the latest trends in church growth. And inevitably the Word
becomes secondary, and our ministries are shaped by other priori-
ties. "No," says John. Christ conquers by the sharp sword that comes
from His mouth. The Word conquers! The gospel triumphs. Do not
be ashamed of the gospel. It is the power of God unto salvation for all
who believe, to the Jew first, and also to the Gentile:

> He speaks and listening to His voice
>   new life the dead receive.
> The mournful broken hearts rejoice,
>   the humble poor believe![2]

And more than that, John says: "he shall rule them with a rod
of iron." That's a reference to Psalm 2:8–9, where the Lord estab-
lishes His Son to triumph over the rebellious nations. "Ask of me,"
the Father says to Him, "and I shall give thee the heathen for thine
inheritance, and the uttermost parts of the earth for thy possession.

---

2. "O For A Thousand Tongues to Sing," *The Trinity Hymnal* (Suwanee, Ga.:
Great Commission Publications, 1990), 164.

Thou shalt break them with a rod of iron; thou shalt dash them in pieces like a potter's vessel."

There is political turmoil on the national stage. Maverick states like North Korea pose a real threat. Russia has become once again an enemy of Western democracy. Islamic terrorism continues to shatter peace. Wickedness seems to go unpunished. Vice is celebrated. Moral confusion prevails. I read this week that there are more LGBTQI+ candidates running for elected public office in the United States this year than ever before. Here's a line to repeat to yourself for the comfort of your soul no matter what the news is. For all the wickedness of the world and tumult of the moral and political landscape right now, here's a truth to preach to our hearts: "And out of his mouth goeth a sharp sword, that with it he should smite the nations: and he shall rule them with a rod of iron." He will rule! He will rule! We can quiet our souls with those words, can't we? He will rule!

Further, John says that, as the ruler of all, "he treadeth the winepress of the fierceness and wrath of Almighty God." Gentle Jesus, meek and mild: He is the agent of the wrath of God, upon whose thigh is written "King of kings and Lord of lords." When the pundits and prophets of doom have only bleak predictions, fill your gaze with a fresh sight of the true and only King. Remember the one who conquers by means of the cross, whose robes are stained by His own blood, and who rides forth, even now, to judge the world in equity.

And look at the effect His riding forth has in verses 17–21. There are two suppers: every single person in history is invited to one of them. Either you attend the marriage supper of the Lamb (that is the subject of verses 6–10, which Dr. Beeke so helpfully expounds in his book on Revelation),[3] or you attend "the supper of the great God" depicted here in verses 17–21. The first is a picture of heavenly celebration. The second is a gory image of utter defeat and everlasting condemnation. The birds of the air are invited to gorge themselves on the corpses of a defeated army. The army is identified in verse 19. It is "the beast, and the kings of the earth, and their armies," who have "gathered together to make war against him that sat on the horse, and against his army." Now understand that this is not a picture of a single final confrontation. This is the perpetual stance of the satanic

3. Joel Beeke, *Revelation*, Lectio Continua Expository Commentary on the New Testament (Grand Rapids: Reformation Heritage Books, 2016).

powers of rebellion and sin. This is the world in which we live, taking up battle lines against the Lord and His anointed.

The final battle for which they ready themselves is never fought. The text simply says that Jesus rides forth on His white horse (vv. 11–16), and then in 20–21, "the beast was taken, and with him the false prophet that wrought miracles before him, with which he deceived them that had received the mark of the beast, and them that worshipped his image. These both were cast alive into a lake of fire burning with brimstone. And the remnant were slain with the sword of him that sat upon the horse, which sword proceeded out of his mouth: and all the fowls were filled with their flesh."

It's a gory image, to be sure. But the message is that Jesus wins. There is no final battle. The world powers of sin and spiritual rebellion, the false religion that deceives and lies to the nations—they all are dispatched to hell as the word of Christ slays those who follow them. If the world will not embrace the promises of gospel mercy that Christ's word brings in life, it must endure the promises of judicial wrath that this same word will bring at the last day. At the conclusion of history, when Christ appears in glory, no matter how fierce and terrible the raging nations appear, Christ the Warrior King need only speak, and judgment shall fall.

The other day I was watching a short film about people who had been unable to see certain colors but who were fitted with special glasses that helped them see the whole spectrum. That's what our passage does: it shows us the full spectrum of color when we've been living in a world of grays. It helps us see the world as it really is. It reminds us that while the nations may gather together against Christ, He cannot be defeated, because He has already won! His robe is already bloodstained! The battle belongs to Him, who triumphed at the cross.

The Triumph of the Church, Christ's Warrior Kingdom (Rev. 20:1–15)

The triumph of the church, Christ's warrior Kingdom, unfolds in four scenes:

Scene One

The first is in Revelation 20:1–3. An angel who holds the keys to the bottomless pit and a great chain, binds the dragon, Satan himself, for a thousand years, throwing him into the bottomless pit, so "that he should deceive the nations no more, till the thousand years should be fulfilled: and after that he must be loosed a little season" (Rev. 20:3). Now, here is a place where we're most in danger of looking out the wrong side of the boat. We get so fixated on the millennium and its meaning that we miss the big idea. We tend to let our fixed dogmatic conclusions about the end times color our reading of the text so that we end up obscuring the truth that ought to stand out most clearly. So let's take another look at the text, looking at it with fresh eyes.

Here is Satan bound—though I am persuaded that he is bound, not at the end of history, as some believe, but bound at the cross. At Calvary, Christ "spoiled principalities and powers, he made a shew of them openly, triumphing over them in it"—in the cross (Col. 2:15). Satan fell from heaven like lightning during the earthly ministry of Jesus Christ, according to Luke 10:18. Jesus came to bind the strong man (Mark 3:27). He could say of the work He was doing "Now is the judgment of this world: now shall the prince of this world be cast out. And I, if I be lifted up from the earth, will draw all men unto me" (John 12:31–32). That is the same message John sees in his vision. Satan is bound and cast down. His power to deceive the nations is curtailed for a thousand years. Now remember, Revelation is "not interested in statistics but in symbols."[4] All the numbers thus far in the book have a symbolic meaning, and this number is no different. Here the thousand years represents the whole period between Christ's comings. And now, John is saying, because He has been lifted up on the cross, He draws all people to Himself, from every tribe and language and nation. What an encouragement these verses ought to be! The devil would like nothing so much as to keep you fearful and cowering at the posturing of egotistical politicians and the perversity of sexual revolutionaries. But the truth is, Satan is not free! He is chained, bound, imprisoned in the bottomless pit. He cannot thwart or hinder the advance of the cause of Christ in the world. John wants us to see Satan's chains and take heart.

---

4. Johnson, *Discipleship on the Edge* (Vancouver, B.C.: Regent College Publishing, 2004), 183.

Scene Two

The next scene is in verses 4–6. John wants us to see the truth about ourselves as Christians, in order to drive the encouragement home still deeper. First, at the end of verse 4, he speaks about those who suffer for the sake of Christ as having come back to life. This, he says, "is the first resurrection." Notice carefully how he speaks to his original readers about it: "Blessed and holy is he that hath part in [present tense] the first resurrection: on such the second death hath no power." This is a blessing John wants his first hearers to enjoy right away, as they hear the message of the book—the first resurrection. This isn't a reference to some kind of physical resurrection of believers at the beginning of an earthly millennial kingdom. Just as the thousand years are symbolic of the whole church age, so the first resurrection is spiritual in nature. It is the new birth. It is regeneration. Jesus talks about it in precisely those terms in John 5:24–25:

> Verily, verily, I say unto you, He that heareth my word, and believeth on him that sent me, hath everlasting life, and shall not come into condemnation; but is passed from death unto life. Verily, verily, I say unto you, The hour is coming, and now is, when the dead shall hear the voice of the Son of God: and they that hear shall live.

Those who trust in Christ and do not bend the knee to the beast, really live. We have the blessedness of resurrection life in a dark and dying world.

And more than that, John wants us to see that, while living, we reign with Christ. Do you see that in the text? Those who came to life, verse 4 and again in verse 6, "reign with him a thousand years." Granted, it doesn't always feel like it to the suffering church on earth, does it? But when believers finish their pilgrimage, they do not go to oblivion, or to some kind of soul-sleep. They go to be with the Lord, who reigns upon His throne. They are swept up into participation in the victory of Christ.

Yes, on earth we suffered and labored and wearied ourselves, often wondering if our labor in the Lord had, in fact, been in vain after all. We sowed in tears. We shed our blood. We gave our lives. But then, one day, death was swallowed up in victory, and though we sowed in tears here, when we go to be with the Lord, we begin, at last, to reap in joy, taking our seats on thrones of our own, beside

Jesus, the great King. And then we get to see from heaven's vantage point what we could see only glimpses of at best on earth — as missionaries penetrate yet another unreached people group for the first time, and new gospel churches are planted in dark cities and neglected communities, and lost sinners are plucked from Satan's snarling maw and brought into the kingdom of God through the patient, faithful, prayerful witness of the suffering church. We get to watch as the world does all it can to hinder the gospel's advance, and again and again, we will see it confounded and overcome as modest Christians go about their lives with gentleness and joy, testifying to Christ's redeeming love.

Now remember that John is writing to Christians suffering under the boot heel of a brutal Roman dictatorship. The politics of the world made life miserable for the followers of Jesus. The church was bleeding and dying, and John himself was in jail for the sake of the gospel. Our current political troubles and our cultural pressures are light and insignificant compared to the difficulties they endured. And to them John says, first, that Satan is bound. He cannot deceive the nations. The gospel will advance, so press on! Then he says, you are alive. Blessed are those who share in the first resurrection! And then thirdly, he says, you will reign with Jesus till the end of the age! Yes, the world makes you slaves and martyrs, but you are really kings! Every act of service, every word of witness — it all extends the reign of King Jesus, and one day you will see that clearly, when you take your seat with Him in the glory that awaits you! So, dear struggling believer in Jesus, do not grow weary in well doing, for you shall reap a harvest in due course if you do not give up!

Scenes Three and Four

And then, briefly, notice the last two scenes in verses 7–15. At the end of the thousand years, Satan is released from his prison and will come out to deceive the nations that are at the four corners of the earth. They are called here "Gog and Magog." Now, again, popular end times theorists try to identify these two powers based largely on their reading of the latest world news: "Are they Russia and China? Are they Islam and America?" Who are they?

The names actually come from the prophecy of Ezekiel, chapters 38 and 39. And they belong to the ancient enemies of God's people.

And that, I think, is John's very simple point. This is not an esoteric warning about who the aggressors in the next global war will be. These are not encoded tips for future American foreign policy. That's not John's point at all. He is simply telling us that the ancient hatred of the world against the church will one day flare up again in a final paroxysm of rage and malice, under the manipulations of Satan. The church will be besieged in a climactic moment of persecution. They will, verse 9, surround "the camp of the saints about, and the beloved city." It's the very same scene described in chapter 19 all over again. It's the final battle. But again, it's a battle that is never fought. The church is besieged by a hateful world. Everything looks bleak. And then Jesus simply wins. Do you see that in verse 9? "And fire came down from God out of heaven, and devoured them. And the devil that deceived them was cast into the lake of fire and brimstone, where the beast and the false prophet are, and shall be tormented day and night for ever and ever."

Jesus wins, do you see, merely by showing up! No shots are fired! Satan is overthrown, and the world in all its malice is summoned to judgment day. There is no strategy of the devil, nor any cunning of men, that can avoid it. And look at verses 11–15. Here is history's end, as creation flees from Christ's presence (v. 11). Everyone who has ever lived is assembled for the final great assize.

Verse 12 says that the great and the small are there. Verse 13 says that the sea, and death, and hades all give up their dead. There is no exception, no exclusions, no free passes. Everyone is here. And books are opened: the books of deeds and the book of life. God has the complete record of our lives written down, as it were, and the name of everyone who believes in Jesus alone for salvation is indelibly recorded. Everyone is judged by "those things which were written in the books, according to their works" (v. 12). And we must see clearly that while hell—the lake of fire—is the sentence passed over those whose deeds condemn them, those who escape do not escape because there are no misdeeds recorded in the books. They escape, rather, because their names are written in the Book of Life. Do you see that in verse 15? "And whosoever was not found written in the book of life was cast into the lake of fire." The only route of escape is to have your name in the Book; it is to believe on the Lord

Jesus Christ alone for salvation. Is your name enrolled on the charter of heaven, as a follower of the Lamb?

When you stand before Christ's tribunal on the great final day, and the books are opened and your life recounted, you will not point to anything in the book of deeds and say, "Jesus, because of this You must accept me." No, you will simply point to your name inscribed in the other book, the Book of Life. It declares that Jesus Himself bought and paid for you by His blood. To be sure, the book of deeds will bear testimony to the reality of your faith, as you grew in obedience to King Jesus. There will be a record of your faithfulness in those books. But your faithfulness will not acquit you. Your imperfect obedience will not save you. But the Book of Life is the ledger of every soul for whom Jesus died. And if your name is written there, you need not fear the moment of your appearance before the great white throne.

Revelation chapters 19 and 20 offer Christians a pair of spectacles to wear to help us see the real world clearly—not the FOX News, CNN-world. Not the Facebook/Twitter world. Not the world of national propaganda and personal boasting. But the *real* world: the world where Christ is king, and Satan is bound, and the gospel advances, and the kingdom of God triumphs! Some of us, I rather suspect, need to put those spectacles back on, and squelch our fear and unbelief, and begin to view reality as it really is, as the great theater of Christ's final victory!

So here is the triumph of Christ, the Warrior King. And here is the triumph of the church, Christ's warrior kingdom. Here's the real world! May God give us grace to see it clearly, and live in it faithfully, till Christ comes! Amen.

CHAPTER 4

Beauty and Glory in Isaiah and Revelation 21

Daniel C. Timmer

There is little doubt that the biblical themes of beauty and glory come to their fullest expression in the Book of Revelation. To affirm this is also to recognize that these themes develop progressively across the biblical canon and in concert with the progressive accomplishment of God's saving work. A study of the relationship between earlier treatments of the themes of beauty and glory and their full and final development at the end of Revelation will bring both of these progressive movements into view and allow us to better understand Scripture's rich unity. With that goal in mind, we will first note some interpretative principles that should guide study of Scripture, and then explore some of the ways that themes from the Book of Isaiah are taken up in Revelation 21.

What Does Interpretation Involve?

While our task here might be described as simply recognizing and explaining relationships between passages that share a common theme, there is more to it than that simple description might suggest. Analyzing such relationships involves the ways that words, concepts, and themes express the meaning of the text; accounting for chronological and historical differences between earlier and later texts; and recognizing theological structures such as the various biblical covenants. Each of these facets of our study requires brief exploration before we continue.[1]

---

1. V. Philips Long notes the inseparability of the literary, historical, and theological facets of Scripture in "Reading the Old Testament as Literature," in *Interpreting the Old Testament: A Guide for Exegesis*, ed. Craig C. Broyles (Grand Rapids: Baker Academic, 2001), 85–123.

Words

While tracing a single word across the canon may give a partial view of what Scripture says about that word (e.g., "beauty"), more than one word or expression can refer to the same idea or thing. Our study of "beauty" should therefore include words (whether originally in Hebrew, Aramaic, or Greek) like fair, lovely, and desirable as well as words like "adorned" that can overlap with those ideas.[2] And since the parts of a text cannot be separated, it is also necessary to recognize ways that our themes intersect other ones.

History

We have already observed that God's self-revelation in Scripture was a progressive, organic process. As a result, readers of Scripture must take account of the historical distance between various texts in at least a general way (books whose authors are named can be dated more precisely than those which are anonymous). This historical distance is inseparable from the need to understand the earlier text in light of the later (Heb. 1:1–2).

Theology

Finally, there is the question of how to properly recognize theological connections between two texts. This is especially pressing if the texts are cast in different literary genres, as, say, the Gospel of Mark and one of Paul's epistles. If texts are from different authors and time periods, the task of connecting them theologically is more demanding, since one text will include some theological categories not present in the other, and vice versa. Despite this diversity, readers of Scripture can have unshakeable confidence that God's Word is a unity and that it finds its full meaning in relation to Jesus Christ (Luke 24; Rom. 1:1–3; 1 Peter 1:10–12), and careful study will eventually lead to a solid understanding of the theology the text expresses.

Unity amid Diversity

In light of these features that God has seen fit to make part of His inscripturated Word, we can expand our initial task description from simply "recognizing and explaining relationships between

---

2. See C. John Collins, "p'r," in *New International Dictionary of Old Testament Theology and Exegesis*, ed. Willem VanGemeren (Grand Rapids: Zondervan, 1997), 3:574.

passages" to something like the following: identifying specific themes presented using a variety of words, taking account of the ways that these themes develop over time and are presented differently in different books, and recognizing how and why they all intersect the person and work of Jesus Christ as God incarnate. This means, on the one hand, that we cannot say that Scripture's many parts simply repeat without change to what other parts of Scripture have already said: we must preserve Scripture's diversity and richness. On the other hand, we must recognize that the ways that God has explicitly connected the parts of His Word so that it forms an intelligible whole must be recognized and followed in our interpretation: we cannot attribute to Scripture a unity less robust than that which it claims for itself.

The Role of the Interpreter and Scripture's Ultimate Author
The fact that Scripture interprets itself does not eliminate our responsibility as readers, who as imperfect, sinful, and limited human beings cannot come to understand Scripture without ourselves becoming involved in the task of understanding Scripture.[3] Because Scripture makes the interrelation of its parts clear in so many different ways, we can learn how to become good interpreters of it by simply reading it with due attention to its literary, historical, and theological facets and with the awareness of our need for God's grace and the Holy Spirit's help in so doing.[4] Indeed, the fact that Scripture is self-interpreting makes it impossible, and even wrong, to shy away from our responsibility as interpreters of it. There is no Reformed equivalent for the Jewish Mishnah or Talmuds that gather authoritative interpretations which infallibly guide our reading and make the task we are describing here unnecessary.[5] Being aware of our dependence upon God for its proper interpretation and practice, we should always undertake the reading of Scripture with the prayer that the Lord would enable

---

3. The Westminster Confession of Faith reminds us that "The infallible rule of interpretation is the Scripture itself" (WCF 1.9).

4. Murray Rae, "'Incline Your Ear So That You May Live': Principles of Biblical Epistemology," in *The Bible and Epistemology: Biblical Soundings in the Knowledge of God*, ed. M. Healy and R. Parry (Milton Keynes: Paternoster, 2007), 163.

5. On the Mishnah, see Jacob Neusner, *The Classics of Judaism: A Textbook and Reader* (Louisville: Westminster John Knox, 1995), esp. 27–28. On the Talmuds, see Adin Steinsaltz, *The Essential Talmud*, trans. Chaya Galai (Jerusalem: Maggid, 2010), 3–8.

us to approach it with reverence, since it is His; with faith and trust, since He is faithful and true; and with humility and expectation, since His Word cuts through all defenses and yet is the means of divine favor and grace for those who tremble at it (Isa. 66:2).

Isaiah in Revelation 21

We are now in a position to explore a few connections between these two books. For practical reasons we will limit our exploration to the use of Isaiah in Revelation 21. Why Isaiah? First, because Revelation 21 starts with a vision of the "new heavens and new earth" that overlaps substantially with Isaiah's unique prediction of the same in Isaiah 65. Revelation 21 also draws on a number of other elements from elsewhere in the book of Isaiah, as we will see.

Keeping in mind the principles of interpretation noted above, we will try to understand how John is interpreting a passage from Isaiah by focusing on what John says, and comparing that with what Isaiah says. Rather than limiting our study to the words "beauty" and "glory" by themselves, or in connection only to their immediate context, we will look at the meaning of the sentences, paragraphs, and sections in which those terms appear.[6] While we could explore the relationship between Isaiah and Revelation by starting with Isaiah and moving forward in time to Revelation, our focus on Revelation makes it equally interesting to begin there, and then to turn to Isaiah. The result is the same in either case, and will allow us to observe how progressive revelation and God's progressive accomplishment and application of redemption work together to inform our interpretation and help us see the glorious fulfillment of God's plan of salvation, as well as His victory over sin and evil, in and through Jesus Christ.

Literary Context: The Book of Revelation

Our focus on part of the Book of Revelation calls for a brief survey of the book's setting and message. The panorama sketched in the Book of Revelation begins in the first century, with John exiled on Patmos, the Roman empire dominating much of the world and claiming unlimited power and glory for itself, and the early church struggling

---

6. Peter Cotterell and Max Turner, *Linguistics & Biblical Interpretation* (Downers Grove, Ill.: InterVarsity, 1989), 77–82.

to remain faithful to her Lord amid persecution by the empire and temptation by the world. John makes clear that these apparently chaotic, dangerous, and uncertain times are emphatically *not* uncertain. Whatever the church might fear, whether in the first century or later, God is *fully* in control, and His will determines all that happens. The vision of heaven in chapters 4–5, for example, shows that God's plan of salvation is fully accomplished, with the Lamb slain and alive again. God the Father, the Author of the scroll in chapter 5, sits enthroned as the sovereign Creator and Ruler of history. Jesus Christ alone has the authority to open the scroll and to execute the Father's will, bringing about His purposes in history.

At the risk of oversimplification, we can say that God pursues two objectives in history, as the book of Revelation surveys it, from John's day until the end: the salvation of His people and the judgment and destruction of all those who persist in rebellion against Him. Salvation has already been accomplished by Jesus Christ, but its application to God's people is not completed until the very end of the book. As an example of this already-not yet tension, note how the saints who died as martyrs are described as "souls" in Revelation 6:9, simply because they are, even today, awaiting the resurrection of their bodies. They also await the final demonstration of God's justice, and hence ask God "how long?" before He will avenge their blood.

Judgment is also progressively realized in Revelation rather than being poured out all at once. We see this in the way that judgment is presented in three overlapping cycles of progressively worsening judgment (seals, trumpets, and bowls) in chapters 6–16; in descriptions of Babylon's fall in chapters 17–19:10; and in the final destruction of God's enemies in Revelation 19:11–20:15. The theme of judgment is tied exclusively to sinners, and should not be confused with the sufferings and persecution of the saints, which the book definitely does not overlook but treats as something fundamentally different. The sharp distinction between the saints and the rest of humanity is reinforced by three interludes that clarify the role of the saints amid God's judgments in chapter 7, chapters 10–11, and the beginning of chapter 20 (7:1–17 precedes the seventh seal; 10:1–11:14 precedes the seventh trumpet; and 20:1–6 precedes the final destruction of God's enemies).

Revelation 21 and its Themes

With this literary context in mind, let's consider the first four verses of Revelation 21.

> And I saw a new heaven and a new earth: for the first heaven and the first earth were passed away; and there was no more sea. And I John saw the holy city, new Jerusalem, coming down from God out of heaven, prepared as a bride adorned for her husband. And I heard a great voice out of heaven saying, Behold, the tabernacle of God is with men, and he will dwell with them, and they shall be his people, and God himself shall be with them, and be their God. And God shall wipe away all tears from their eyes; and there shall be no more death, neither sorrow, nor crying, neither shall there be any more pain: for the former things are passed away.

What themes are present in this short section? Obviously the new heavens and the new earth are central, but other themes intersect that primary one: marriage as a metaphor for the relationship between Christ and His church in verse 2; the presence of God with His people in verse 3; and the removal of pain, grief, and death in verse 4. Let's consider each of these in more detail.

New Heavens and New Earth

Revelation

The new heavens and new earth is something of an umbrella-theme which envelops or is made up of the other themes in this section. Indeed, the best way to understand this very far-reaching image is to fill in its content with what follows in the rest of chapters 21 and 22. But at least one point should be made before we do so: the "new heavens and new earth" presupposes the disappearance, or better, the renewal, of the "old" (cf. 2 Peter 3:10). In Revelation, this process is part of the Day of the LORD in the judgment of the sixth seal (Rev. 6:12–17; cf. 20:11). Revelation makes clear that the fallen world is terribly marred by sin, and that the vast majority of humanity follows one false god after another. God's gracious plan to redeem His people and bring the entire creation to the end-goal for which He created it means that rather than totally destroying it, He will purge it of sin and renew it. The "destruction" of the "old" heavens and earth is thus not absolute.[7]

Isaiah

Not surprisingly, Isaiah 65:17, the passage that is connected to Revelation 21 by the phrase "new heavens and new earth," makes essentially the same point. There too we find sharp discontinuity between old and new: "the former things shall not be remembered nor come to mind." In fact, this discontinuity is so great that God uses the language of creation to describe how He brings about the new heavens and new earth in 65:17–18 (Hebrew *bārā'*). But creation in this context means something other than complete and absolute discontinuity, since in verse 18 God also creates "Jerusalem and its people," both of which already exist.[8] Continuity and radical newness coexist.

The Absence of Sin and Consequent Absence of Pain and Death

Revelation

What follows in our passage unfolds in more detail what this new heavens and new earth will be like. It is interesting that the first description of the new heavens and new earth in Revelation 21 involves something that it is not, something that is absent from it. *Sin* will no longer be present in the renewed cosmos! This is beautifully captured by the phrase "there was no more sea." When the sea is used symbolically elsewhere in Revelation, it has several overlapping senses that are tied to the concept of evil.[9] It is the realm from which the beast emerges in 13:1, while in the vision of heaven in 4:6 there is "something like a sea" whose glass-like appearance before the throne shows that it no longer offers any resistance to God's will. This point is made emphatically in 15:2, where the sea is the surface on which those who have gained victory over the beast stand and praise God in 15:2.

The absence of sin from the new heavens and new earth is, to say the least, a radical change from the present cosmos as we know it!

---

7. G. K. Beale, *The Book of Revelation*, NIGTC (Grand Rapids: Eerdmans, 1999), 1040.

8. John Oswalt, *Isaiah 40–66*, NICOT (Grand Rapids: Eerdmans, 1998), 657.

9. G. B. Caird, *A Commentary on the Revelation of St. John the Divine* (New York: Harper & Row, 1966), 65–68.

The devil, fallen angels, empires, and individual human beings all participate in a cosmic act of ongoing rebellion that seeks to remove God from His throne and put oneself there instead. It is helpful to view this reality in relation to the ideology and projects of the Roman Empire in the first century A.D., which defined not only the general context in which John wrote but which had seen him exiled to Patmos.[10] The empire is almost certainly what is signified by the beast in chapter 13, which misuses religion to control its subjects. It is probably also behind the image of the prostitute "Babylon" in chapter 18, which depicts an empire extracting as much benefit and control as possible from its economic relationships.[11] It is also possible that the famous figure 666 in 13:18 refers to the Hebrew gematriac value of "Neron Qesar" (N=50, R=200, W=6, N=50; Q=100, S=60, R=200, for a total of 666), infamous for his violent persecution of Christians near the end of his reign.[12]

The Roman empire of John's day constantly pursued absolute power, and did so by mixing religion, politics, and conquest. One might sum up its official worldview as follows: "The world and all its inhabitants belong to our gods, including our emperors—worship and submit to them!" Not only did common opinion among the elite hold that the Roman empire "was universal and willed by the gods,"[13] but from the time of Caesar Augustus onward, there was an imperial cult dedicated to the worship of dead and, eventually, of living emperors. Augustus had his own temple built before his death to honor him as Jupiter Julius, and after his death he was officially declared to be a god by the Roman senate.[14]

10. Robert H. Mounce concludes from Rev. 1:9 that "Apparently the Asian authorities had interpreted his [John's] preaching as seditious and removed him from the mainland in an attempt to inhibit the growth of the early church;" *The Book of Revelation*, NICNT (Grand Rapids: Eerdmans, 1998), 54–55.

11. So Richard Bauckham, *The Theology of the Book of Revelation*, New Testament Theology (Cambridge: Cambridge University Press, 1993), 36.

12. A few manuscripts read 616, which is the gematriac value of Caligula; see Mounce, *Revelation*, 261–62, who reminds us that this is "a Hebrew transliteration of the Greek form of a Latin name," Neron Qesar, without the *yod* in Qesar, and reading a *waw* with the long *o* of Neron but omitting the e- and a-vowels.

13. Peter A. Brunt, "Laus Imperii," in *Roman Imperial Themes* (Oxford: Clarendon, 1990), 291, cited in Warren Carter and Leo G. Perdue, *Israel and Empire: A Postcolonial History of Israel and Early Judaism* (London: T & T Clark, 2014), 227.

14. Everett Ferguson, *Backgrounds of Early Christianity*, 3rd ed. (Grand Rapids: Eerdmans, 2003), 208.

At first glance this might seem rather distant from the concerns of the Apostle John, but from the time of Augustus onward, Asia, the location of the seven churches whom Christ addresses in Revelation's opening chapters, "had been the strongest center of the imperial cult."[15] At the same time that Revelation was written, the Roman historian Suetonius "describes how 'lord god' became [the emperor] Domitian's standard title in correspondence and conversation, how images of this emperor in Rome had to be of a certain weight of gold or silver and how various architectural embellishments proliferated as means of encouraging worship of Domitian."[16] It was also during the reign of Domitian "that failure to honor the emperor as a god became a political offense and punishable."[17] Even Roman coins were used to promote the deification of the emperor by ascribing to him divine titles or by depicting him as Rome's mediator.[18]

Against this backdrop, Revelation 21 does indeed present us with a radically new, purified world in which such self-deification no longer exists. The creation of the new heavens and new earth involves the abasing of human pride and glory in order to make way for the full revelation of God's glory. The removal of sin also undoes the curse of vanity that lies upon the cosmos as a whole (Rom. 8:21) and completes the liberation of the children of God from sin's guilt, power, and curse. In this renewed cosmos, sin is absent. *Entirely* removed! Even though strictly speaking this is only an absence, it is a beautiful and glorious one!

In the book of Revelation, the cause of sin's removal is twofold. The first cause is salvific: the Lamb of God in chapter 4 has redeemed by His blood "people for God from every tribe and tongue and people and nation" (Rev. 4:9; cf. 1:5–6), and their robes are made white in His blood (7:14). The second reason that sin is absent from the new

---

15. Ferguson, *Backgrounds*, 603.

16. M. Reasoner, "Persecution," in *Dictionary of the Later New Testament & Its Developments*, ed. Ralph P. Martin and Peter H. Davids (Downers Grove, Ill.: IVP Academic, 1997), 907–14.

17. Mounce, *Revelation*, 17.

18. One finds on a coin minted under Julius Caesar (49–48 BC) images of an elephant trampling a dragon (a "traditional symbol of power") and of priestly implements including the *culullus* (ritual cup), *aspergillum* (sprinkler), axe (for killing the animal), and *apex* (priest's cap with pointed wood top). See the images and their explanation at http://www.humanities.mq.edu.au/acans/caesar/Career_Representing Power.htm

heavens and new earth is more sobering: God's righteous judgment destroys all who persist in rebellion against him. When confronted by God's wrath, the great and powerful of the earth will ask in terror, "Who can stand?" (6:17). The answer, of course, is "No one." God destroys the destroyers of the earth (11:18), and His wrath brings down all those who oppose His will: sinners who do not repent in the three cycles of judgment in chapters 6–16, symbolic Babylon in chapters 17–18, or the beast, the false prophet, and those with them in chapter 19 (vv. 17–21). All God's enemies fall once and for all before the Word of God who rides a white horse and leads "the armies of heaven" (19:11–16).

Isaiah

Isaiah describes a world very similar to John's. The world, inclusive of Judah in Isaiah's day, is characterized by rebellion against God's will, by worship of other gods, and by a proud, autonomous attitude that leads individuals and nations to treat others, and even God Himself, as things to be used for their own self-centered ends.[19] By the late eighth century, when Isaiah's ministry began, Judah had wandered far from God. Her kings did not show a consistent commitment to following God's will or trusting in His ability to deliver them from the dangers posed by the nations around them. Further, the beliefs and behavior of king and people alike had far too much in common with other nations.

The non-Israelite nations, for their part, were characterized by violence against one another, by regular aggression against Judah (something in which the northern kingdom of Israel occasionally participated, 2 Kings 14:8–14), by a pride that knew no bounds, and by worship of other gods. The kings of the Assyrian empire, which often threatened Israel and Judah, expressed this well in their royal annals. Sennacherib (reigned 705–681 B.C.), who threatened Jerusalem during the time of Isaiah's ministry, described himself as follows:

---

19. Geerhardus Vos notes that God's holiness and glory are His preeminent attributes in Isaiah, and both are attacked by the attitude of the world. "Some Doctrinal Features of the Early Prophecies of Isaiah," in *Redemptive History and Biblical Interpretation: The Shorter Writings of Geerhardus Vos*, ed. Richard B. Gaffin Jr. (Phillipsburg, N.J.: P&R, 1980), 278.

Sennacherib, great king, strong king, king of Assyria, unrivalled king, pious shepherd who reveres the great gods, guardian of truth who loves justice…perfect man, virile warrior, foremost of all rulers, the bridle that controls the insubmissive, [and] the one who strikes enemies with lightning.[20]

In the same breath he asserts that "The god Aššur, the great mountain, granted to me unrivalled sovereignty and made my weapons greater than (those of) all who sit on (royal) daises."[21]

Projects of empire and domination like these constituted a dogged effort on the part of these nations to control as much as possible of their surroundings and their destiny. This was true both of large empires like Egypt, Assyria, and Babylon, and of smaller, regional powers like Moab, Edom, and the Syrians. In short, non-Israelites and Israelites alike were convinced of their fundamental right to self-determination and manifested no desire to recognize or glorify their God and Creator.

Like John, Isaiah insists that God will bring an end to all sin, especially sins which involve outright self-glorification and a corresponding refusal to recognize God's unparalleled glory. His prophetic vision is large enough to encompass the entire world, but also complex enough to include both judgment and salvation, as in Revelation. The northern kingdom habitually refused to walk in God's ways, and was exiled to Assyria as punishment for her sins in 722.[22] Despite that object lesson, the southern kingdom of Judah continued to wander from God and His law, and in Isaiah's day there was only a remnant left (Isa. 1:9; a future, believing remnant appears in 4:2–3; 11:11, 16; 24:6 and other passages).

Yet the remnant would prove to be the seed from which a new Israel grew, and this remnant is ultimately defined by its relationship to the Suffering Servant. This is clear from the new focus on restored Israel in Isaiah 54 that appears as the fruit of the final and climactic description of the work of the Servant of the Lord in chapter 53.[23] The

---

20. A. Kirk Grayson and Jamie Novotny, *The Royal Inscriptions of Sennacherib, King of Assyria (705–681 BC), Part 1,* RINAP 3/1 (Winona Lake: Eisenbrauns, 2012), 32.

21. Grayson and Novotny, *The Royal Inscriptions of Sennacherib,* 32.

22. There were in fact several deportations, some before and some after 722; see K. Lawson Younger, Jr., "The Deportations of the Israelites," *Journal of Biblical Literature* 117 (1998): 201–27.

23. Oswalt, *Isaiah 40–66,* 413.

same pattern of judgment and salvation also holds for the nations, who will be punished in the near future but will (in part) turn to the LORD and worship Him with His people in the "last days." For example, Isaiah 19 puts Egypt's punishment in the near future side by side with its salvation in the last days, when it will enjoy the same salvation and blessing as Israel. Accompanied by the undoing or removal of the pride that is at the heart of human sin and rebellion, the arrival of the new heavens and new earth that Isaiah anticipates is filled with YHWH's glory (Isa. 6:3) so that "the LORD alone will be exalted in that day" (Isa. 2:11, 17).

Biblical-theological reflections
The fact that Revelation was composed roughly eight centuries after the Book of Isaiah, and that it could look back on the beginning of the last stage period of redemptive history (the "last days," Acts 2:17; Heb. 1:2), means that its message is clearer than Isaiah's at various points. Revelation makes clear that the Israel of prophecy finds its fulfillment in the church, which is composed of both Jews and Gentiles who are no longer separated by the Sinai covenant (Isaiah 66 and a few other passages come close to saying the same).[24] John's apocalypse also identifies Jesus in terms that overlap almost entirely with Isaiah's depiction of the Suffering Servant, who bears the sins of His people. Finally, Revelation makes clearer than did Isaiah that the Day of the LORD comes about progressively, in an already-not yet way. In the last days, God brings increasingly sharp warnings against sinners and calls His people to exercise faith as they await His deliverance at the end of time.[25]

New Jerusalem

The new Jerusalem is the first element in Revelation 21 whose *presence* is essential to the new heavens and new earth.

---

24. Barry G. Webb, "Zion in Transformation: A Literary Approach to Isaiah," in *The Bible In Three Dimensions*, ed. David J. A. Clines, Stephen E. Fowl and Stanley E. Porter, JSOTSup 87 (Sheffield: JSOT, 1990), 79.

25. Bauckham, *Revelation*, 40.

Revelation

Despite the architectural detail that follows later in chapter 21, the new Jerusalem is not made of bricks and mortar, but of *people*. In the verses we are considering, John describes this group, which is none other than the glorified church, in three ways. The first, "as a holy city" (cf. Isa. 52:1), emphasizes the sinless nature of those who will inhabit the new heavens and new earth. The second, "coming down from heaven," hints at the fact that the glorified church has not received its full inheritance until God brings them, in resurrected and glorified bodies, "down" into the new heavens and new earth.[26] The third, "as a bride adorned for her husband," is probably a case in which Isaiah served as a template for John's description of his vision.[27] In Isaiah 62, the prophet speaks of Jerusalem's salvation in words of unsurpassed beauty:

> And the Gentiles shall see thy righteousness, and all kings thy glory: and thou shalt be called by a new name, which the mouth of the LORD shall name. Thou shalt also be a crown of glory in the hand of the LORD, and a royal diadem in the hand of thy God. Thou shalt no more be termed Forsaken; neither shall thy land any more be termed Desolate: but thou shalt be called Hephzibah, and thy land Beulah: for the LORD delighteth in thee, and thy land shall be married. For *as* a young man marrieth a virgin, *so* shall thy sons marry thee: and *as* the bridegroom rejoiceth over the bride, *so* shall thy God rejoice over thee (vv. 62:2–5).

Of the many points that merit sustained attention here, we can deal only with a few. None other than God Himself gives the salvation that renders His redeemed people glorious (62:2) and beautiful (62:3), yet He delights in her all the same (62:4). Further, Isaiah uses the idea of marriage (cf. 61:10), and the flexible Hebrew word behind it (*ba'al*), to capture three dimensions of this salvation: the LORD's unchallenged possession of the land (*Be'ulah*) from which exiled Israel had been estranged; Zion's sons entering a permanent and sacred relationship with her (*be'alu*); and God rejoicing over His now-sinless covenant partner as a bridegroom rejoices over His bride. Although

---

26. Beale, *Revelation*, 1041.
27. So Beale, *Revelation*, 1044.

here Isaiah stops short of affirming outright that God is His people's husband in this passage, that idea appears in Isaiah 54:5.[28]

Even so, John's description of the intimate and unbreakable relationship between Christ and His church goes still further, and uses the image of Christ as the husband of His people in a way possible only on the basis of God's fully completed and applied work of redemption.[29] All these elements contribute to John's later statement that the church "had the glory of God" in Revelation 21:10. She has become "like" God when she sees Him as He is (1 John 3:2), and so shares in a measure of, and reflects, His inexpressible glory.

Isaiah

Although it does not strike every note that John's apocalypse does, Isaiah's presentation of the new Jerusalem includes elements not found in the book of Revelation, which is not surprising given its greater length. One notable example is Isaiah's emphasis on renewed Jerusalem at points in redemptive history prior to the very last stage of eschatology on which John focuses in Revelation 21.

In the eschatological vision of Isaiah 2, for example, after God has exalted His temple and His name above every other, the nations flow to Zion because the word of the LORD has gone out from it. The implication that God's people are acting in some sort of missionary capacity accords well with the role of Israel and the Servant of the LORD as a light "to the nations" elsewhere in Isaiah (Isa 42:1–4, 6; 49:6; 60:3; cf. Deut 4:6).[30] This means that history has not yet ended, for the gospel is still being preached.

As another example, in Isaiah 35 the "glory" (kabōd) and "splendor" (hadar) of the LORD appear in the desert as He accompanies His redeemed people in a second exodus out of the exile of sin and its consequences all the way back to the gates of a sinless Zion (35:2,

---

28. "Master" is also a possible sense there, as in Isaiah 26:13, but the context of 54:1–4 presents YHWH-as-ba'al in contrast to Zion as either widowed or desolate/unmarried, making "husband" much more likely.

29. Contrast the Sinai covenant context of Hosea's use of the marriage metaphor, Hosea 2:1. The point is that even the marriage metaphor can have different denotations or connotations depending on its context, and the progress of redemption determines its limits.

30. Willem A. M. Beuken, Jesaja 1–12, HThKAT (Freiberg: Herder, 2003), 93, notes the relevance of Deuteronomy 4:5–8 in this context.

8–10).[31] This stage of redemption also stops short of the consummation, for elsewhere Isaiah's description continues further, and reaches almost to the very end of God's redemptive work that John describes in Revelation 21.

Biblical-theological reflections
Once again, Revelation's chronological position as the last book of the canon, composed in the light of the first coming of Jesus Christ, lends clarity and precision to its treatment of themes presented earlier in Isaiah. John's development of Isaiah's themes is natural and uncontrived, meaning that he adds nothing to them that is inconsistent with them. At the same time, there is genuine progress in God's ongoing revelation and in His work of salvation.

Divine Presence
Our final theme, divine presence, appears in a variety of words and images in Revelation and Isaiah.

Revelation
The affirmation elsewhere in Revelation that there is no temple or tabernacle in the new heavens and new earth makes clear that Revelation 21:3 is not simply affirming that the tabernacle or temple will once again be among God's glorified people. That was something of a status quo in Israel, beginning with the tabernacle in the wilderness and continuing through Solomon's temple before the exile and the second temple after it. Rather than being a structure or a place, the tabernacle in Revelation 21 is God's *activity* of being present with His people, as the text goes on to explain (and cf. 21:22).

God's presence with His people by His Holy Spirit has already been inaugurated in the New Testament through the gift of the Spirit in union with the risen Christ.[32] Both Paul (Eph. 2:20–22) and Peter (1 Peter 2:5) use the metaphor of a living temple to describe the people of God animated and united by this one Spirit. But prior to believers' perfection upon their death, and all the more so prior to the full completion of God's work of redemption as depicted here, this divine

---

31. The nations meet a radically different fate in Isaiah 34, which contrasts with chapter 35.
32. So, correctly, Beale, *Revelation*, 1047.

presence cannot be perfectly realized with the existence of indwelling sin (here and now) or without resurrection bodies (for the saints in heaven who await the resurrection). The divine presence here in Revelation 21, by contrast, is full and cannot be improved upon as the full application of redemption accomplished.

Isaiah

If we trace this theme back to Isaiah, we find that the prophet almost always connects God's presence to the temple, whether in the present (Isa. 37) or in the future (Isa. 2:2–5; 56:7; 57:13; 60:7, 13). There are a few indications, however, that when God's work of salvation is complete, His presence will transcend a physical building in which non-Israelites will one day worship Him as part of His people (Isa. 56:7). The first hint is the elevation of the "mountain of the LORD's house above the mountains" in chapter 2, which clearly is not simply a physical relocation.[33] There is also a blunt rejection in Isaiah 66:1 of any temple thought to contain God's presence.[34] A third hint appears in the expectation in chapter 11 and in 65:25 that God's temple mountain will fill the whole earth. The fourth and final indication that divine presence will one day be far more than a local phenomenon in a temple appears in Isaiah 24. This passage is intriguing enough to demand a closer look.

Isaiah 24 presents a vision of worldwide judgment for the sins that have defiled the earth (24:4–5). Divine wrath against sin is so great that it brings an end to the existing creation, with the earth being split apart, staggering, and falling, never to rise again (24:19–20). The next unit, however, announces that this judgment will be followed by salvation. After God destroys His enemies, earthly or heavenly, His glory will be revealed in such a way that the moon and sun will be ashamed by comparison. This revelation reaches its high point when God's glory "will be before his elders" (Isa. 24:23), the LORD Himself will serve a lavish meal "for all peoples," and will do away with death itself (Isa. 25:6–8).

---

33. Matthieu Richelle, "L'affluence des nations à Jérusalem en vue du salut," in *L'amour de la sagesse: Hommage à Henri Blocher*, ed. Alain Nisus (Charols: Excelsis, 2012), 109.

34. Daniel C. Timmer, *Creation, Tabernacle, and Sabbath: The Sabbath Frame of Exodus 31:12–17; 35:1–3 in Exegetical and Theological Perspective*, FRLANT 227 (Göttingen: Vandenhoeck & Ruprecht, 2009), 147.

There are several reasons to see this scene as an amplification or escalation of the Sinai covenant meal recorded in Exodus 24. There Moses, Aaron, Nadab, Abihu, and seventy elders of Israel ascended Mount Sinai, "saw the God of Israel" and "ate and drank" in His presence. Note the following links between the two scenes:

- the first exodus from slavery in Egypt corresponds typologically to Isaiah's second exodus that consists of liberation from sin and the experience of salvation;
- in both passages the elders are prominent as representatives of the people;
- they see or are in the presence of God and His glory (*kabōd*, in Exod. 24:16–17);
- the contexts of both passages involve a meal on the mountain that God has consecrated.[35]

The connections in Isaiah 24–25 to the covenant ceremony in Exodus suggest that in Isaiah 24–25 God is establishing a new covenant with His people. This new covenant shelters them from His judgment against sin, removes sin's curse and so makes possible the death of death, and allows them to experience His glory without being consumed.[36]

Biblical-theological reflections

Standing at the end of the process of special revelation, John can speak in more detail than Isaiah of judgment, redemption, and final salvation. The unsurpassed divine presence that John describes is inseparable from progress in the accomplishment and application of redemption, which, once completed, allows an experience of God's presence that surpasses what was possible in Eden (probation), during the Sinai covenant, or even under the New Covenant prior to

---

35. Beuken, *Jesaja 13–27*, 337–38.

36. At that point in God's progressive revelation and accomplishment of His saving purposes, however, Isaiah can hardly say more. What he says, however, is fully compatible with the text's Christological fulfillment, because the divine author supervenes the human author. Cf. Daniel C. Timmer, "Reading the Old Testament as Part of a Two-Testament Witness to Christ," in *Interpreting the Old Testament Theologically: Essays in Honor of Willem VanGemeren*, ed. Andrew Abernethy (Grand Rapids: Zondervan Academic, 2018), 95–108, following Kevin Vanhoozer, *Is There a Meaning in This Text? The Bible, the Reader, and the Morality of Literary Knowledge* (Grand Rapids: Zondervan, 1998), 265.

believers' glorification. This is beautifully captured by the marriage supper of the Lamb, announced in Revelation 19, which celebrates the complete fulfillment of God's plan in the full and final salvation and deliverance of His people and looks forward to the church's eternal, intimate communion with her Savior.

Conclusions

Our study of Isaiah's relationship to Revelation 21 has verified a number of guidelines and basic beliefs that we set out for ourselves at the beginning. These include:

- the importance of recognizing thematic, rather than single-word, links between passages;
- that Scripture speaks with one voice even as it speaks in different literary genres—Isaiah in prophecy, Revelation mostly in vision or apocalyptic;
- that Scripture speaks with increasing clarity as progressive revelation and the accomplishment of redemption advance; and
- that the full meaning of all texts, Old Testament and New Testament alike, is tied to one or another facet of Christ's person and work.

Since the goal of interpretation includes more than getting the method right, it is fitting to bring together the themes and redemptive-historical developments that we have noted in some concluding experiential and practical observations.

First, whatever situation we find ourselves in, Isaiah and Revelation both insist on the absolutely definitive fact that God alone is King. *All* that happens is determined by His royal, omnipotent will and word, and that will for His people gives them rich grace now and unspeakable glory later.[37]

Second, the experience of salvation opens our eyes to the beauty and glory of God in Christ as manifested in all His works. The triune God demonstrates His beauty and glory as He brings about His perfectly wise, gracious plan to glorify Himself as Creator (Rev. 4:11), Redeemer, and Consummator. This means that the beauty and glory of the last things are ultimately *derivative*—they are a reflection of

---

37. Recall the importance of the opening visions of the resurrected and ascended Christ as King of kings in Revelation 1.

God's intrinsic beauty and glory (note how God Himself is Israel's glory in Isa. 60:19, and how the glory of the new Jerusalem is God's glory, Rev. 21:11). In light of this, every believer is obliged and called to pursue ever deeper experience of that glory now in part, and one day in full measure, "in the face of Jesus Christ" (2 Cor. 4:6).

Finally, wherever we find it, beauty is properly understood and appreciated only when we see God as its source. Geerhardus Vos observed with his typically acute insight that "beauty irreligiously appreciated detracts from the glory of Jehovah."[38] Contrariwise, Bill Edgar argues that when it is properly understood, "beauty is a manifestation of the reality of another scheme of things, the author of being and of salvation."[39] The proper reflection and expression of beauty by God's creatures involves "being conformed to all that is involved in a living, grace-filled, covenant relation to God the creator and redeemer."[40] May God grant us to live that way for His glory and our everlasting joy!

---

38. Vos, "Doctrinal Features," 282.

39. William Edgar, "Aesthetics: Beauty Avenged, Apologetics Enriched," *Westminster Theological Journal* 63 (2001): 115.

40. Edgar, "Aesthetics," 120.

TOPICAL STUDIES

CHAPTER 5

The Signs of the Times

David P. Murray

Horrendous hurricanes, enormous earthquakes, fierce fires, phenomenal floods, dangerous diseases, virulent viruses. Almost every day that we open our newspapers or click on news websites we see these and similar headlines. We sense these events are growing in number and seriousness. Over the last 12–18 months especially, we have witnessed multiple record-breaking hurricanes, devastating fires, and overwhelming flooding, and that's just in the USA. The rest of the world has also experienced similar tumultuous events. So much so, that many are asking, "Are these signs of the end? Are these indicators that the end is nigh?"

It's not just Christians who are asking these questions. Even the secular *New York Times* published an article entitled, *Apocalyptic Thoughts Amid Nature's Chaos? You Could Be Forgiven.* It began:

Vicious hurricanes all in a row, one having swamped Houston and another about to buzz through Florida after ripping up the Caribbean.

Wildfires bursting out all over the West after a season of scorching hot temperatures and years of dryness. And late Thursday night, off the coast of Mexico, a monster of an earthquake.

You could be forgiven for thinking apocalyptic thoughts, like the science fiction writer John Scalzi who, surveying the charred and flooded and shaken landscape, declared that this "sure feels like the End Times are getting in a few dress rehearsals right now."

And just last month darkness descended on the land as the moon erased the sun. Everyone thought the eclipse was awesome, but now we're not so sure—for all the recent ruin seems deeply, darkly not coincidental.[1]

The article then enters scientific re-assurance mode to dampen our fears: "If you thought that, you would be wrong, of course. As any scientist will tell you, nature doesn't work that way." All these hurricanes, fires, earthquakes, etc., are normal, within the usual bounds of frequency, severity, and so on.

A liberal theologian, Christiana Zenner Peppard of Fordham University, was also quoted to convince readers that any dalliance with apocalyptic thinking exiles you to the fringes of thoughtful society:

> With unexpected cataclysmic weather events, people across time and space have always looked for explanations…. The fact is it is attractive to certain segments of the population to look at unforeseen apocalyptic-style events as fitting into a particular kind of narrative.[2]

Yet, the eerie sense that these events have some greater significance abides. "While the sense of some gathering apocalypse is not sending people into bunkers," says the *Times*, "it lingers even in secular minds, if not always consciously." Ahmed Ragab, a professor of science and religion at Harvard, admitted that the cumulation of disasters is affecting people, with many concluding that there is a message of doom in it all. The "signs of the times" are making people think about the times and what these signs mean. Is this the end-times? If secular sources are looking at these signs and wondering what they mean, then surely we as Christians should think even more seriously, solemnly, and deeply about these events and ask, "Is this the end-times?"

The disciples asked similar big questions at the beginning of Matthew 24. In verses 1–2, Jesus predicted the destruction of the temple:

> And Jesus went out, and departed from the temple: and his disciples came to him for to shew him the buildings of the temple. And Jesus said unto them, See ye not all these things? verily I say

1. Henry Fountain, *Apocalyptic Thoughts Amid Nature's Chaos? You Could Be Forgiven*, New York Times, September 8, 2017, https://www.nytimes.com/2017/09/08/us /hurricane-irma-earthquake-fires.html.

2. Fountain, *Apocalyptic Thoughts Amid Nature's Chaos*.

unto you, There shall not be left here one stone upon another, that shall not be thrown down.

A short time later, the clearly shaken disciples approached Jesus privately as they overlooked the temple from the Mount of Olives and enquired: "Tell us, when shall these things be? and what shall be the sign of thy coming, and of the end of the world?" The secular world cannot answer these big questions about end-time signs, but the Lord can and does in the following verses. His teaching reveals three characteristics of these signs of the times:

- The Signs are Continuous but Intensifying
- The Signs are Varied but United
- The Signs are Spectacular but not Speculative

We'll now explore Christ's teaching on the signs under these headings.

The Signs are Continuous but Intensifying

There are two major mistakes that people make when thinking about the signs of the times. The first is *to believe that all the signs will be fulfilled in the future*. They read Matthew 24 and say, "This is all about the end of the world." But that's not possible, because there are references to events that were clearly fulfilled in the years immediately after Jesus's death and resurrection. For example, in verse 16, we read, "Then let them which be in Judaea flee into the mountains." Obviously this is not speaking about the very end of the world. Rather, this was fulfilled about 70 AD with the fall of Jerusalem. So, when we read these chapters we cannot be thinking only about the end-times.

A second mistake is *to believe that all these signs were fulfilled in the past*. Some people look at certain references to times and places that were clearly fulfilled in the first century AD and say, "Well, that means all these signs were fulfilled then." But that doesn't fit the evidence. For example, in verse 14 we read about the gospel going out to all the world: "And this gospel of the kingdom shall be preached in all the world for a witness unto all nations; and then shall the end come." That had not happened in the first century AD. Arguably, it hasn't even happened now. Also, verse 21 warns, "For then shall be great tribulation, such as was not since the beginning of the world to this time, no, nor ever shall be." Although what happened to Jerusalem in 70 AD was terrible, it in no way matches this description. Bad though Jerusalem's fall was, there were much worse events in history before that, and there has certainly been much worse since, even in the past century.

We want to avoid both of these mistakes—that all these signs will be fulfilled in the future, or that all these signs have been fulfilled in the past. So, if it's not all future and it's not all past, what is it? The key is to take a slightly closer look at the question the disciples ask in verse 3, which reveals that it's really two questions. First, "When shall these things be?" Second, "And what shall be the sign of thy coming, and of the end of the world?" For the disciples, when they heard that Jerusalem was going to fall, they thought, well, that's the end of the world. If the temple falls, the world ends. So, when they are asking these two questions, what they had in mind was one moment, one event, one period in time.

But, Jesus's answer indicates that He saw these two questions as referring to events at two different times. What the disciples thought was one time, Jesus saw as two different times. There is the fall of Jerusalem, and there is something bigger coming later. Jesus used the fall of Jerusalem as a type of what would happen at the end of the world. He was teaching that all of these terrible events that are about to happen in Jerusalem, all of that is a prophetic picture of what will happen to a far greater degree towards the end of the world. So, He was using a smaller imminent event, the fall of Jerusalem, to make a picture prophecy of a more distant and more momentous event. He was using the palette of Jerusalem's fall to paint a picture of what's going to happen at the end of the world.

We do this ourselves at times. You may remember that when the American forces went into Afghanistan post-9/11, and ran into some early difficulties, the news headlines were "Quagmire" or "Another Vietnam." The media were referring back to events in Vietnam during the 1960s and 70s to help people understand what they thought was happening in Afghanistan in the early 2000s. In Europe, we speak of some big political challenge facing a Prime Minister or President as "their Waterloo." Again, this is using a past event to picture present and future events. That's what Jesus was doing here.

The signs of the times, then, begin with Jerusalem in 70 AD, but continue to the end of time with increasing intensity. Jesus was saying, "Look at what's going to happen to Jerusalem, and from that you will be able to tell what the whole future of history will be like in an increasing measure." These signs are continuous but intensifying. They are not all past and they are not all future. They are past, they are present, and they are future. But it's not a straight line, as if we can expect these things to be the same all throughout history. The chapter indicates a crescendo of intensity throughout world history that will finally come to a great climax at the end. If you want to picture this graphically, it's not one dot in the past, it's not one dot in the future, and it's not a dotted line from past to future that stays on the same level. The dots are increasing in frequency and intensity throughout all ages until at the end of time one big dot covers the whole universe.

We can see this intensification in Matthew 24. Look, for example, at the following verses and the highlighted words in italic:

"And ye shall hear of wars and rumours of wars: see that ye be not troubled: for all these things *must* come to pass, but the end is *not yet*" (v. 6).

"For nation shall rise against nation, and kingdom against kingdom: and there shall be famines, and pestilences, and earthquakes, in divers places. All these are *the beginning of sorrows*" (vv. 7–8).

"And this gospel of the kingdom shall be preached in all the world for a witness unto all nations; and *then* shall the end come" (v. 14).

"The end is not yet...these are the beginning of sorrows...and then shall the end come." These are different time markers that coincide with the beginning, the increase, and the climax of the signs. That's why we say, *the signs are continuous but intensifying*.

What does this mean for us practically? First, it means that *we must be looking out for the signs of the times*. We must not ignore the events that are happening in world history. If the *New York Times* is thinking about them, then surely Christians should be thinking even more seriously about the events God is ordering in His world for His divine purpose. We should be reading the news with Matthew 24 lenses and filters, so that we are discerning the signs of the times as being part of a divine pattern that began in Jerusalem, that's increasing throughout world history, and that's going to come to a great climax at the end. We observe them, we let them impact us, but we don't just brush them off.

Second, it means that *we don't panic*. Many people, even in the church, see these signs of the times and rush out with blogs, books, sermons, etc., and go into an alarmist, get-into-the-bunkers, survivalist mode. No, this chapter teaches us that while we should be aware of and sensitive to the signs of the times, there's no need to panic, there's no need for hysteria. This is just normal, part of the ordinary everyday outworking of God's purpose and plan. It's been happening throughout history and it's going to continue to the end of history. So observe, think seriously, but don't panic. That's the message of these continuous but intensifying signs.

The Signs are Varied but United

Remember the *New York Times* headline which spoke of "chaos"? If all we do is read our newspapers or browse the web, that's the conclusion we will come away with: the world and history is totally out of control. It's cataclysmic, meaningless, and purposeless. Without a biblical filter, that's really the only conclusion we can come to. But it's not the conclusion we come to when we use the Word of God to help us interpret these signs.

Although the signs are very different in certain features, yet they are united in purpose and meaning. I want to show you two outlines of world history that we have in Matthew 24. As this is one of the most complex chapters in the Bible, to see a big-picture visual of it will help us understand the details better. After the question and answer session between the disciples and Jesus in verses 1–3, Jesus gives us history in broad outline (vv. 4–14) and then history in more detail (vv. 15–31). It's like "Lecture One: Summary," then "Lecture Two: Details."

History in Outline (vv. 4–14)
- Apostasy (5)
- Wars (6–7a)
- Natural disasters (7b)
- Persecution (9)
- More apostasy (10–12)
- Gospel (14)

History in Detail (vv. 15–31)

- Tribulation (14–22)
- Apostasy (23–27)
- Deterioration (28)
- Supernatural signs in nature (29)

Jesus gives us a summary of history in verses 4–14. These are the things we can expect to characterize history, occurring with increasing intensity throughout the ages. Then He teases out some of the more salient details in the second section (vv. 15–31). The detailed look is possibly much more focused on their relevance to God's people. Perhaps we can say that, on balance, the second section places more emphasis on the spiritual side of these signs.

In passing, I want to just highlight one of the detailed signs, the deterioration in verse 28, which is often viewed as rather mysterious: "For wherever the carcass is, there the eagles will be gathered together." Jesus is saying that as these signs unfold, what we're going to get eventually is a carcass of a society, a society that's been so broken down by sin and judgment that all that's left is just a stinking, rotten, vile carcass of an animal. I don't think you can get a better description of where we are as a society today. If we compare where we are today with where we were even twenty or thirty years ago, then who can deny the increasing putrefaction, deterioration, and corruption? Who would have thought that marriage would be so redefined? Who would have thought that what used to be regarded as a shameful perversion would now be both promoted and preferred? When we look at some of the judgments issued by our courts and the laws being proposed, who can deny that what we are looking at is the decomposing remains of a once glorious beast? When we look at these things, we ask, "What events could be worse?"

And yet, it's not chaos. Although the signs are so varied, different, unexpected, and seem to be chaotic, Jesus was saying, "I know all of this is going to happen. None of these different signs takes me by surprise. They don't unsettle me. I expected all of these varied signs."

Also, although varied, they are actually united. Think about what we are doing when we put up a sign. We are saying, "Follow that sign to where it is pointing." When we read the varied signs in Matthew, they are not pointing in all sorts of different directions; they are all pointing to a single destination. And that destination is *God*. Indeed, we should probably not call them "the signs of the times" but "the signs of God." That's where these signs in all their variety and diversity are pointing us. They are God-centered signs. Starting from the fall of Jerusalem and continuing throughout history, they are all pointing to God.

For example, there are *signs pointing to the grace of God*, such as the gospel going out into all the world and people being saved. Second, there are *signs pointing to opposition to God*. The tribulation, the persecution, and the deterioration are God-centered, in that they point to the enmity of the human heart to God. Think of some of the laws that are proposed or passed; when you actually look at them rationally, they defy rationality. There is no logic or reasonable explanation behind them. There is no evidence that these things are for the good of human society or human flourishing. Indeed, all the evidence is to the contrary. And we scratch our heads and ask how such an idea or proposal can even be thought of, never mind that it has millions of people supporting it and millions of dollars promoting it. You are not going to find a reason in the realm of logic. You will only find the explanation in the enmity of the human heart. These trends are expressions of unbridled hatred and hostility toward God. So, even the worst things in society are pointing toward God by showing us people's opposition to Him. The very existence of God and His moral law is such that it stirs up opposition to God and all that He stands for. Third, there are *signs of God's judgment*, things like volcanos, earthquakes, wars, and so on.

These signs are varied but united in their God-centeredness. At the end of Christ's *outline* of world history, He speaks of the end of the world (v. 14). There's only one "end" of the world, not two or three or four. At the end of Christ's *detailed* look at world history He associates His return to this world with that end. Again, there is only one return of Christ, not two or more. "Then the sign of the Son of Man will appear in heaven…and they will see the Son of Man coming on the clouds of heaven with power and great glory" (v. 30). This is the final event presented in Christ's detailed look at church history. The end of the world and the coming of Christ happen together. There is one end, one return, and it's all about one Person. There have been many signs pointing to God, but now there shall be one unmistakable sign of God: "They will see the Son of Man coming on the clouds of heaven with power and great glory." This is the ultimate sign in power and glory. It's the ultimate sign *geographically* in that every eye shall see Him. It's the ultimate sign *chronologically*, because there are none after it. It's the ultimate sign *impactfully* because, although many ignore the signs of God now, this is one sign that no one can or will ignore. Every eye shall see the Son of Man coming in the clouds of heaven. There will be one end, one return, one Person, who will dominate the end of world history.

The United Call of These Signs

All of these varied signs throughout history and at the end of history are pointing to God and are urging, "Let God impress you. React and respond to God. Do something about your relationship with God." And at the end of these signs is God's ultimate sign, when there is no longer any opportunity to respond. Every eye will see Him, but there will be no opportunity to repent and believe. It will be too late. This last sign of God will impact everyone but change no one. These signs are varied but united in their God-centeredness—and in their urgent call.

Will you be ready? Have you used the signs to direct yourself to God, to get right with God, to prepare to meet your God? Are you seeing the signs, or are you blinding your eyes, closing your ears, shutting off your heart? Well, there is a day coming when you will close your eyes no longer. Every eye will see, every ear will hear, every heart will bow, but it will be too late to make an eternal difference.

The Signs are Spectacular but not Speculative

As the *New York Times* article demonstrated, whenever there is a series of what looks like end-time signs, there are always attempts to put the pieces together and figure out, "Is this the end?" Another example that the *Times* article referenced was a Tweet which was widely shared: "The solar eclipse was on the 21st. Hurricane Harvey showed up on the 25th and started flooding the 26th. Now look up Luke 21:25–26." And what does it say? "And there will be signs in the sun, in the moon, and in the stars; and on the earth distress of nations, with perplexity, the sea and the waves roaring; men's hearts failing them from fear and the expectation of those things which are coming on the earth, for the powers of the heavens will be shaken."

This is an example of the kind of speculation that we want to avoid. This is numerological speculation that moves people away from the divine intention in all these signs. Signs are not given to help us speculate. Yes, they are spectacular, they impress us, they knock us off our feet, they make us think, but they are ultimately given to lead us to action, not speculation.

You'll notice that Jesus says in this very passage: "But of that day and hour knoweth no man, no, not the angels of heaven, but my Father only" (Matt. 24:36). These are among the most unbelieved words in the whole Bible. It couldn't be clearer: "No one knows." Not even the Son of Man, in His human nature, can look at these signs and work out, even approximately, the date of the end. These signs are not given to encourage speculation, to help us predict the date of Christ's return, but to help us prepare for Christ's return. And that should be our focus: not prediction but preparation. That's where Jesus goes after He's given His outline and the details of world history. He says, "Prepare for the end of Jerusalem" and "Prepare for the end of the world."

Seeing the signs of the times should spur our preparation for the end of time (vv. 32–33). First, Christ warned His own generation to be prepared for the end of Jerusalem (vv. 34–35).[3] And second, He called all generations to prepare for the end of the world (vv. 36–50), with the former (end of Jerusalem) being a type of the latter (end of the world). He addressed His present audience and called them to be prepared for the destruction of Jerusalem and then said, as it were, "Now the rest of you people who are going to live after this generation, you who are going to see all these signs, you get ready for a far greater end, the ultimate end, the end of all ends. Be prepared for the end of the world, and of that day no one but the Father knows."

The signs of the times can't be used to date Christ's return. Although they will all be fulfilled, we don't know all the details of what, where, when, and how. Regardless of whether they satisfy our desire to know the date, use the signs to get ready, to prepare. For example:

> "So likewise ye, when ye shall see all these things, know that it is near, even at the doors!" (v. 33)

---

3. "This generation" means the Jews of Christ's time. "All these things" means the end of Jerusalem.

Also:

> But as the days of Noah were, so shall also the coming of the Son of man be. For as in the days that were before the flood they were eating and drinking, marrying and giving in marriage, until the day that Noe entered into the ark, and knew not until the flood came, and took them all away; so shall also the coming of the Son of man be. (vv. 37–39).

Jesus recalls Noah's day and says, "Don't be as unprepared as that generation":

> Watch therefore: for ye know not what hour your Lord doth come (v. 42).

And again:

> Therefore be ye also ready: for in such an hour as ye think not the Son of man cometh (v. 44).

He's given lots of teaching about the signs of the end, but He drives it all to this repeated point: "Prepare to meet your God, get ready. I've given you abundant signs; now, use them."

I was listening to a radio program in which a meteorologist was looking back to the 1920s and the hurricanes that used to hit Florida. He was saying that no one then had any early warning signs. Nowadays we have tracking from ten days out, five days out, three days out, two hours away, and so on. The news issues warnings, and sirens are sounded. But in the 1920s there were no weather satellites; there were no meteorological or media warnings. People were just going about their Florida business when—boom!—totally out of the blue a hurricane hit. Hundreds of thousands of people died over the years in these hurricanes.

But we are blessed not just with warnings about hurricanes but with warnings about the end. Jesus is saying to us, "If you blind your eyes to these signs, you are as good as dead. You are just going to be like these people who die without warning and you have no excuse. You've had plenty of early warning signs."

Conclusion: Taking the Signs Seriously

So how do we prepare for the end? First, *get serious*. Sometimes, when we see the religious speculation around the latest signs, we almost laugh at how ridiculous the predictions are. It's extreme; it's way "out of left-field." We're much more sensible and rational. But the danger is that we won't pay *any* attention to the signs. These signs are saying, "Sober up, get serious." When hurricane Irma was coming through the Florida Keys, a pub owner was posting videos on social media. "One day to go," then "One hour to go." It was all a laugh a minute. He was a social media star. "We're going to get some guys around, have a few beers, have a great time," he predicted. And then the signal went blank. The videos stopped. The Tweets stopped. He wasn't seen for something like 24 hours. And when the internet service came back up, this man's face was very different than it was 24 hours earlier. He was bedraggled, his clothes were ripped, he was bruised. It was as if he'd seen a ghost. No one is going to be laughing on the last day. So, we should prepare for it seriously, thoughtfully.

Second, *get reliable information*. Floridians are news addicts in hurricane season. Where is the hurricane coming from, what's its track, where should we go for safety? They are picking up every piece of information, trying to get reliable information, so that they can take appropriate action. That's what this passage calls us to do. Get reliable information! We have it all here in God's Word. Matthew 24 is not the only passage that deals with the end times. We should be studying these passages, comparing God's Word with what's happening out there. Use God's Word to get reliable information, to understand what's happening, and then take appropriate action.

Third, *get your house in order*. When hurricanes are coming, people take lots of precaution to protect their properties, especially by shoring up their weak points. They put up shutters and boards and tie things down. They take evasive action to get their house in order. The signs of the times tell us to get our house in order too, especially as the signs intensify towards the end. Find out where your weak points are, seek resources—prayer, the Word, the means of grace—to strengthen yourself so that you may be able to stand strong in the tumultuous day.

Fourth, *get away from danger*. Flee the wrath to come. If you have not already fled to Christ, there is no better day than today. Some people are trying to bank on their interpretation of the signs. "They are not as bad they will be," they reassure themselves. "Things have not yet happened as I speculated they should happen, and therefore I've still got time." What a miscalculation this could be! Such "experts" are banking on prophetic interpretation and spiritual math that, admittedly, none of us is very good at. Remember that even though the Old Testament prophets predicted Christ's first coming, so few in Israel had any idea when Jesus came that He was the ful-fillment of the Old Testament. Are we any better than they were in figuring out such things?

It's far safer to flee by faith to Jesus Christ. Get to higher ground— to the rock that is higher than we are! Get on your knees and pray for yourself and your family. Speak to your family about these things. When was the last time we warned them that the end is near? Jesus was very conscious of the need to live as if the end was imminent. The ultimate message of these signs is "Live (and preach) as if Christ died yesterday, rose today, and is coming back tomorrow."

CHAPTER 6

Heaven on Earth

Derek W. H. Thomas

What is heaven like? Surprisingly, even though belief that heaven exists is central to Christianity, the answer to this question can be surprisingly vague, even from those whose Christianity is Bible-based and orthodox. Will there be books? Libraries? Travel? Music? Will it be *new* music or music we loved in this life? Will we eat? Will there be animals? Will we sleep? Will we have different skills from the ones we have now?

Some questions might seem trivial, though I would argue they are not, since the answers define the nature of our existence in heaven. Some questions are deeply sensitive and puzzling. Since Jesus expressly tells us that there will be no marriage in heaven (Luke 23:43), will we know our spouses as "former" spouses? Will there still be a bond that is like no other?

Before we proceed any further, we need to define with far greater precision what we mean by the term "heaven." What happens to a believer after he dies? "Today," Jesus told the dying thief, "shalt thou be with me in paradise" (Luke 23:43). The Shorter Catechism addresses this issue this way:

Q. 37. What benefits do believers receive from Christ at death?

A. The souls of believers are at their death made perfect in holiness, and do immediately pass into glory; and their bodies, being still united in Christ, do rest in their graves, till the resurrection.

In addition to the dying thief passage, the Catechism alludes to the fact that there exists right now a "general assembly of the church of the firstborn, which are written in heaven" (Heb. 12:23). It also cites Paul's words to the Corinthians that to be absent from the body is to be present with the Lord (2 Cor. 5:8) and his word of assurance to the Philippians, written from his confinement in Rome, that he is uncertain as to whether he will be released (so he can come and visit the Philippian church), or executed, in which case he will "be with Christ" (Phil. 1:23).

This assurance of heaven after Christians die is central, theologically and pastorally, and has been and remains the basis of sure Christian hope in the face of death. It is surprising therefore—puzzling even—that in his new biography of Paul, N. T. Wright repeatedly claims that the gospel is not "we go to heaven when we die." To be sure, it not *the gospel* but it is a fundamental consequence of the gospel.[1]

One of the most cited examples of such Christian confidence of heaven after death is that of Robert Bruce, a great old Scottish Covenanter who witnessed so greatly and boldly for the Lord.[2] On morning of August 1631, this old saint of God, who had lived only for his Lord, rose to have breakfast with his family. Having eaten an egg, he asked his daughter to get him another one.

> Suddenly he changed, and started meditating. And then, with an attitude of deep meditation, he said, "No, hold, daughter; my Master calls me." He asked for someone to bring him the family Bible. But when they brought the Bible, he found that he had lost his sight, so he asked them to turn to the eighth chapter of the epistle to the Romans and find *verses 38 to 39*. "Now," he said, "have you found the place? Read it to me." So they read, "I am persuaded that neither death nor life shall be able to separate me from the love of God which is in Christ Jesus." "Now," he said, "put my finger on the place." Having put his finger on the place, he said, "Then God be with you, my children. I have breakfasted with you this morning; this evening I shall sup with my Lord in glory." And he died. Hallelujah! "Let me die the death of the righteous, and let my last end be like his!"[3]

What precisely do we mean when we say, "heaven"? Are we talking about a conscious existence ten seconds after we die? Are we referring to what theologians call the "intermediate state"? Or are we

---

1. N.T. Wright, *Paul: A Biography* (San Francisco: Harper One, 2019), 7–9 (cf. 75, 221, 401, 403–404, 406).

2. Not to be confused with King Robert Bruce (or Robert the Bruce), 1274–1329.

3. Iain Murray, "Robert Bruce: Standing Fast in Dark Days," in *A Scottish Christian Heritage* (Edinburgh: Banner of Truth, 2006), 56–57.

talking about the final state of things, post-resurrection of the body, after the constellation of events that occur either just before or just after the Second Coming—what the Bible refers to as "the new heavens and new earth"? These are two very *different* places and realities. I am persuaded that I will be in heaven *immediately* after I die, but I shall not spend eternity only in this realm, wherever it is, but I believe I shall also dwell on a new earth canopied by new heavens (Isa. 65:17; 66:22; 2 Peter 3:13; Rev. 21:1).

It is precisely the distrust of the material universe, and all that this implies for our existence now and hereafter, that led Augustine (a one-time follower of Manichean thought) in his *City of God* to so contrast the two cities (the *City of God* and the *Earthly City*) that readers are left with one conclusion: that this world is a place of captivity. For Augustine, there is no place for temporal things to be considered "good in themselves." This denial surely runs counter the New Testament's insistence that such things as marriage (intimacy) and food are essentially good things for which one should give thanks to God (cf. 1 Tim. 4:3; Heb. 13:4). One of the reasons why the Reformers were urged to marry was to counter what was in part a residue of Augustinian thought, namely the medieval Roman Catholic church's view that celibacy was a higher form of sanctification.[4]

A Biblical Glimpse of Heaven

How much of the nature of the resurrected life does the Bible disclose to us? Without becoming overly speculative and crossing over into fantasy, we can at least follow certain clues to tease out some features of the life to come after the Second Coming of our Lord Jesus Christ.

Ultimately, heaven is about having perfect communion with the triune God. In eternal glory, we who are believers will enjoy knowing, seeing, loving, praising, and communing with God and, above all, glorifying Him forever. We will experience feasting at His right hand where there are pleasures forevermore. In heaven we will enjoy perfect salvation. We will be completely delivered from the enticements of Satan, the allurements of the world, our own old nature, and yes, from sin itself. We will be as holy as our Savior Himself, and we shall see Him as He is. All evil will be excluded from heaven

---

4. Further on this theme, see William Edgar, *Created and Creating: A Biblical Theology of Culture* (Downers Grove, Ill.: IVP Academic, 2016), 220–29.

and all good will be included. In heaven, there will be no more tears, pain, sorrow, night, death, curse, or temptation.

In heaven, we will engage in perfect activities. We will worship God with much praise and singing. We will be engaged in the service of God and in exercising authority with Him in ways we cannot now imagine. We will enjoy having blessed, God-centered fellowship with the saints and angels beyond a level that we knew during our lives. And we will receive eternal education in the depths of the riches of God's amazing grace. And finally, we will engage in holy, heavenly, spiritual, and physical rest—resting in the triune God and His amazing salvation forever.

What glorious bliss this shall be when our mortality shall put on immortality and our corruption shall put on incorruption, and we shall ever be with the Lord!

Beyond this essence of what heaven is primarily about, many other questions remain: Will I grow in my knowledge—continuously, eternally? And since our sight of the exalted Jesus is the heart of this new existence, how *precisely* will this take place given that He continues to exist in a risen *body*, one that does not possess the property of ubiquity, but rather, a body that is confined to a specific location in space and time? Does this imply that we will need go to where He is in order to see Him rather than be surrounded by His *physical* presence? And since we have mentioned space and time, will our existence in the new earth be one of temporal sequence and spatial proximity?

All these questions grow out of the fact that the final glimpse of the eternal human existence of the redeemed is given in terms of a new city, a temple, a garden, and a new earth (Rev. 21:1–3, 10).

A City

Augustine's two-fold *City of God* and the *Earthly City* parallels the use of Jerusalem and Babylon in Revelation to represent the metropolises of grace and evil, respectively. Babylon is the "the great whore that sitteth upon many waters" (Rev. 17:1). Babylon has been the enemy of God and His people from the time of Genesis 11—the erection of the idolatrous ziggurat and the curse of communication that followed. Babylon was the traditional enemy of God's people; it looms in her history and finally becomes the place where the Israelites were exiled. Babylon represents the evil of all cities in opposition to God.

And Revelation's reference to the seven hills (17:9) is a way of saying that Babylon represents Rome.

In contrast, the new Jerusalem descends from heaven from God, representing that redeemed city (Rev. 21:2). She too is represented as a woman, but not a whore like Babylon, but a beautiful, pure bride (Rev. 19:7; 21:2, 9). It is this city that pilgrims have longed to enter since the time of Abraham: "For he looked for a city which hath foundations, whose builder and maker is God" (Heb. 11:10).

A Temple

"And I saw no temple therein: for the Lord God Almighty and the Lamb are the temple of it" (Rev. 21:22). Throughout most of the Old Testament, God dwelt in a Tabernacle-temple. In fact, the idea of God's presence as a sanctuary starts in Eden. This garden functions as a temple because God is there, walking about in the "cool of the day" (Gen. 3:8). Eden is a garden-sanctuary where God dwells with His people.[5]

One singular difference between life in this aeon and life in the new earth is the absence of a temple, since the whole of the new creation is (in one sense) a temple. The omnipresence of the Almighty and of the localized presence of the Lamb are the temple, namely, the *presence of God in redemptive terms.*

A Garden

The Bible envisions the eternal state to be a restoration of Eden. The new Jerusalem has the waters of life flowing through it (Rev. 7:17; 22:1–2; 21:6). And deeply significant is the fact that the Tree of Life is there for the healing of the nations (Rev. 22:2, 7; 22:14, 19):

> And he shewed me a pure river of water of life, clear as crystal, proceeding out of the throne of God and of the Lamb. In the midst of the street of it, and on either side of the river, was there the tree of life, which bare twelve manner of fruits, and yielded

---

5. For a full analysis of the theme of temple in Scripture, see G. K. Beale, *The Temple and the Church's Mission: A Biblical Theology of the Dwelling Place of God*, New Studies in Biblical Theology (Downers Grove, Ill.: IVP Academic, 2004), and G. K. Beale and Mitchell Kim, *God Dwells Among Us: Expanding Eden to the Ends of the Earth* (Downers Grove, Ill.: InterVarsity, 2014). This chapter is indebted to many of Beale's insights.

her fruit every month: and the leaves of the tree were for the healing of the nations. (Rev. 22:1–2)

Adam and Eve lost their right to the Tree of Life through their wanton disobedience (Gen. 3:22–24), and along with them the entire human posterity (Rom. 5:12–14). And so the narrative of redemption pictures the restoration of fellowship with God in terms of a restoration of the Edenic existence, a renewed Garden-city, teeming with life and fruitfulness (Isa. 49:10; Ezek. 47:1–12; Zech. 14:8). As the original Eden had been teeming with life, the new Edenic state will also be characterized by eschatological life.

A New Earth

John describes a vast city of enormous proportions and security. And what he describes is in one sense fantastical and surprising—a cube, of which each side measures 1,400 miles (Rev. 21:15–17)! The walls are two hundred feet thick, signifying a city that is as vast as it is safe. But it remains an image. John is presenting large numbers, but what lies behind the image of the city?

In Eden, God commissions Adam and Eve to find fulfilment in worshiping Him. God's purpose is to make His presence known in all the earth. Humanity's priestly task in Eden—a task that culminates in spectacular failure—is to keep guard over the Garden by obeying God's word. The mandate to explore and subdue the earth is a command to turn the earth into a Garden-sanctuary. The failure of Adam and Eve sets up the story of the Old Testament with its central feature of the Tabernacle—reminiscent of an architect's scale-model of God's presence with His people and His provision for their sin.

Christmas is a temple story. In Jesus, God's temple is personified. Jesus *is* the temple. The child born in the manger is "Immanuel" meaning "God with us" (Matt. 1:23; cf. Isa. 7:14; 8:8). It is echoed in Revelation 21:3: "And I heard a great voice out of heaven saying, Behold, the tabernacle of God is with men, and he will dwell with them, and they shall be his people, and God himself shall be with them, and be their God." Curiously, John saw no temple in the city; at least, no *physical* temple: "But I saw no temple in it, for the Lord God the Almighty and the Lamb are its temple" (v. 22). This is because Jesus, in fellowship with His redeemed people, embodies the temple.

A Brave New World

What John describes using colored pictures is a place of purity and perfection. "And there shall be no more curse" (Rev. 22:3). Because Jesus was made a curse for us (cf. Gal. 3:13), there is nothing left of the curse in the new city-temple.

It is difficult to imagine a world without sin, but we do long for it. We have an instinct that desires something other than the here and now. "What I would, that do I not" Paul says (Rom. 7:15). There is always this sense of "wanting" in us—that the way things are now is not what ought to be, or even will be:

- I know what I want—to be free from sin's down-drag on my life and the life of others.
- I know what I want—to live in a place where there's joy and happiness and fulfilment.
- I know what I want—to be who I was intended to be.

When sin is no more, sin's pain will also be no more. Pain is a consequence of the curse. Not all pain is bad. Some is positively beneficial. Without pain, we would not know that fire can burn us. It is a good instinct to pull our hand away. It is unclear whether we will experience this kind of pain in the new heaven and earth. Perhaps we will feel the sense of touch, the sharpness of an edge, the heat of a fire, the comfort of a chair, or the softness of a bed.

But there will be no cruel pain, no pain that causes regret and loss. Those tears are wiped away (Rev. 21:4). God, who puts our tears in a bottle (Psa. 56:8), reassures us of His tender comfort and declares that there will be no tears of pain—this kind of pain—in the world to come. None!

Heaven, the final state of it, is a *safe* place. There are no dangers left on the outside to threaten those who occupy this garden-city-temple. The gates of the city are open (Rev. 21:25). There is no fear of attack. Danger is eradicated. The Dragon will be locked in the bottomless pit never to threaten again.

Safety is what is meant by the otherwise enigmatic statement: "and there was no more sea" (Rev. 21:1). The point is not that there will be no oceans. Some, lacking the sensitivity required in interpreting apocalyptic genre, have suggested that the new heaven and new earth will lack all forms of water. Others have suggested that there will be an absence of salt-water but not of natural, fresh water. This misses the symbolism intended. The sea in biblical times was a hostile place. Despite having access to the Mediterranean, the Jews were not a sea-faring people. Thus, in Daniel, monsters rise from the sea (Dan. 7:1–8), something which is echoed in Revelation when a beast of the sea appears (Rev. 13:1). The sea is where Leviathan, the sea-monster, resides (Job 3:8; 41:1; Ps. 104:26). No such ogres will occupy the seas of the new earth.

And who will be found in the new heaven and the new earth? The "nations," the redeemed from every tribe and people and tongue (Rev. 21:24, 26). The mandate of the Great Commission, reflecting the promise given to Abraham at the very beginning, was to make disciples of "all nations" (Matt. 28:19; cf. Gen. 12:2). On the Mount of Olives, Jesus carefully explained to the disciples that the Second Coming could not occur until the gospel was preached in all the nations (Matt. 24:14). And in the end, they will come to the city-garden-temple of the new heaven and new earth from every tribe and people-group. They will enter the city's gates and worship the Lord there. And presumably, their ethnic identity will remain apparent as a sign of God's multifaceted grace put on display.

Of considerable interest at this point is Isaiah's closing prophecy in chapter 60. Here the prophet foresees a time when the wealth of the nations is drawn to "Israel" (60:1–7, especially verse 5). In Isaianic terms, this wealth is described in terms of camels, gold, and frankincense (60:6–7). And the ships from Tarshish arrive carrying Israel's children because God has made them "beautiful" (Isa. 60:9). Once more, the heavenly future is described as a city whose gates are permanently open to allow the wealth of the nations to flow in (60:10–13).[6] The depiction continues in terms that describe the city as just and glorious (60:15–18).

Perhaps the most telling feature of this city for our purposes is that there will be no need for sun or moon because the Lord Himself will be the "everlasting light" (Isa. 60:17–22).

Obviously, knowing how John uses Isaiah 60 is deeply significant if we are to unravel the ultimate focus of this passage as a description of heaven, or more specifically, the *new heavens and the new earth*.

---

6. Alec J. Motyer, *The Prophecy of Isaiah: An Introduction & Commentary* (Downers Grove, Ill.: InterVarsity Press, 1993), 494–97.

It is to this new earth that Isaiah the prophet seems to be alluding in the closing chapters of his prophecy.

From Image to Reality

Richard Mouw argues that what is in view in John's use of Isaiah 60 in Revelation 21 is that the new earth will continue to employ the cultural mandate:

> But the Holy City is not wholly discontinuous with present conditions. The biblical glimpses of this city give us reason to think that its contents will not be wholly unfamiliar to people like us. In fact, the content of this City will be more akin to our present cultural patterns than is usually acknowledged in discussions of the afterlife.[7]

Mouw concludes that the world to come—the new *earth*—will have aspects of *continuity* with our experience of existence in this life. And it is the same idea—though in apocalyptic terms—that John conveys in the closing chapters of Revelation. Though "there shall be no more curse" (Rev. 22:3), there will be continuity. Because Jesus was made a curse for us (cf. Gal. 3:13), there is nothing left of the curse in the new city-temple.

A New Earth

There are important principles involved in thinking about the final state as a new earth. Christianity affirms the material order. God creates a physical world and flesh-and-blood human beings. We should not be surprised, therefore, that the new order will also be a material order with redeemed human beings comprised of flesh and blood. Few truths are more central to Christianity than the physical incarnation and resurrection of the body of Christ. In the consummation, we will once again inhabit physical bodies, localized in space and time, in an environment suited to our physicality. There is every reason to believe that we will experience the new order spatially *and* temporally.

---

7. Richard J. Mouw, *When the Kings Come Marching in: Isaiah and the New Jerusalem* (Grand Rapids: Eerdmans, 2002), 20. Cited by William Edgar, *Created and Creating*, 228.

Animals in heaven?

To highlight this issue of continuity between the world we know and the world to come, let's ask the simple question, "Are there animals in heaven?" God intends to create a new heaven and a new earth and everything that belongs in such an environment will be a part of it. God is going to re-fashion His fallen creation. The question about animals raises therefore another, and more important question: *what kind of heaven are we expecting*? It is often suggested that the reason why animals are *not* in heaven is because they do not have souls. As we saw earlier, this line of reasoning may be misguided. It displays a Greek or Platonic understanding of soul rather than a biblical one. What distinguishes humans from other life forms in the opening chapter of the Bible is not so much the possession (or lack) of *a soul*, but the fact that human beings are made in the "image of God" (Gen. 1:26–27). Take a passage like Isaiah 11:6–9:

> The wolf also shall dwell with the lamb,
>   and the leopard shall lie down with the kid;
>   and the calf and the young lion and the fatling together;
>   and a little child shall lead them.
> And the cow and the bear shall feed;
>   their young ones shall lie down together;
>   and the lion shall eat straw like the ox.
> And the sucking child shall play on the hole of the asp,
>   and the weaned child shall put his hand in the cockatrice' den.
> They shall not hurt nor destroy in all my holy mountain:
>   for the earth shall be full of the knowledge of the LORD,
>   as the waters cover the sea.

Wolves and lambs, goats and leopards, lions and calves, children and snakes—are these merely metaphors of an anticipated better future? Is Isaiah merely giving us a picture of the coming rule and reign of the Messianic King—a "child" and "son" upon whose shoulders the government shall rest, and whose name is "Wonderful, Counselor, Mighty God, Everlasting Father, Prince of Peace" (Isa. 9:6)?

Or is the prophet depicting the spread of Messiah's rule, as mainline *postmillennialists* believe? The metaphors of peaceful coexistence of wild animals would then function as a way of describing the spread of the gospel across the world.

Or is Isaiah's portrait of a restored Eden meant to convey precisely what it says—a world in which the curse of sin is removed and God's creation exists in the harmony and peace of its original state? And if so, the new earth is going to be like the original creation, with all its variety of animals, birds, and fish. If the new earth will have topography reminding us of the Serengeti Plains, the English Cotswolds, or Rocky Mountain National Park, then will it not also include all the wildlife that currently inhabit these regions, including the Pyrenean Ibex, the Caribbean Monk Seal, and the Tasmanian Tiger—animals that are currently extinct? Uncertainty about some of the details need not prevent us from thinking about broader principles and expectations.

Exploration and Inquiry

Perhaps a surer way to inquire about the life to come is to ask the following: for what purpose was humankind created in the first place? The answer is found in the so-called "cultural mandate": "And the Lord God took the man, and put him into the garden of Eden to dress it and to keep it" (Gen. 2:15).

As we hinted at earlier, not all creation was paradise. Humankind was given work to do, to subdue the earth and bring it under His lordship. Things have been made a million times worse because of the opposition and frustration that now manifests itself in creation. The ecological crisis is a result of sin. But even in paradise, Adam and Eve were to work to bring about order and beauty.

This might suggest that in the new heaven and earth, exploration and discovery will continue to be a feature of life—of eternal life, harnessing the universe for the glory of God. A host of related ideas are involved:

- our minds will continue to expand as knowledge increases
- the new heaven and new earth will not be a regression to primitive life, requiring the reinvention of the wheel or the rediscovery of DNA
- scientific and geographical exploration (to name but two disciplines) may continue

Will the discovery of information be easier in the new heaven and new earth? Perhaps. It is difficult to outline the effects of sin on the process of discovery and knowledge. The debilitating effects of memory loss, faulty reasoning, and self-interest alone have catastrophic consequences for the process of discovery and investigation. Free from this contagion, just think what possibilities for advancement there will be! Is it not likely that God intends for us to discover and grow in our human advancement in the world to come rather than be given masses of new information at once?

Rule and Dominion

Exploration, discovery, and creativity are all aspects of rule, exercising dominion over the created order. Just as Adam was told to exercise a kingly *dominion* over the original creation (Gen. 1:28), Christians in the new heavens and earth will also exercise dominion. They will reign over the new creation as vicegerents of the Creator. In the new heavens and new earth, Christians are going to reign with Christ. Writing to Timothy, Paul cited a trustworthy saying: "For if we be dead with him, we shall also live with him: If we suffer, we shall also reign with him: if we deny him, he also will deny us" (2 Tim. 2:11–12).

Elsewhere, Paul asks: "Know ye not that we shall judge angels?" (1 Cor. 6:3). What does this mean? Perhaps, he meant that we will join in the condemnation of fallen angels, but the context suggests that Paul has in mind the holy angels. Since these angels have no sin, what possible judgment could there be? The Greek verb for "judge" (*krino*) also means "to rule, or govern." It may be that the redeemed elect, created and re-created in God's image (angels not being created in God's image), will rule over all creation, including God's exquisite angels. These splendid creatures are ministering spirits created to grant aid to human beings (Heb. 1:14; c.f. Ps. 34:7; 91:11).

When the disciples asked an embarrassing question about greatness in the kingdom of God, Jesus responded: "Ye are they which have continued with me in my temptations. And I appoint unto you a kingdom, as my Father hath appointed unto me; that ye may eat and drink at my table in my kingdom, and sit on thrones judging the twelve tribes of Israel" (Luke 22:28–30).

We read of ruling and assessing, suggesting that we are to expect an extraordinary future. We are, of course, only scratching the surface: "Eye hath not seen, nor ear heard, neither have entered into the heart of man, the things which God hath prepared for them that love him" (1 Cor. 2:9; quoting Isa. 64:4).

CHAPTER 7

Jesus Believed in Hell:
The Modern Christian's Dilemma

Derek H. W. Thomas

Is it possible to believe in Jesus and not believe *everything* He said? Of course, the answer is *Yes*! Many affirm that they believe the Sermon on the Mount, for example, but do *not* affirm certain other particulars attributed to Jesus in the Gospels, like His teaching on hell.

Of course, people who say things like this have, in all likelihood, never actually read the Sermon on the Mount, since less than two dozen verses into it we find Jesus warning those who call their brother "fool," that they will be "in danger of hell (*Gehenna*) fire" (Matt. 5:22). Moreover, the Sermon closes with a warning about a road "that leads to destruction" (Matt. 7:13). Even so, the liberal theologian Nels Ferré can still claim, "whether Jesus taught eternal hell or not is uncertain," a claim which John Blanchard considers "at odds with the evidence."[1]

The view depicted by Ferré is widely held, where folks think of Jesus as some kind of leader, a moral teacher, a man with peculiar insight and wisdom and worthy to be heard and in some sense followed, but ultimately fallible. This was expressed as a famous "trilemma" formulated by "Rabbi" John Duncan (1796–1870) in his *Colloquia Peripatetica*: "Christ either deceived mankind by conscious fraud, or He was Himself deluded and self-deceived, or He was Divine. There is no getting out of this trilemma. It is inexorable."[2]

---

1. John Blanchard, *Whatever Happened to Hell?* (Darlington, England: Evangelical Press, 1991), 129.

2. John Duncan, *Colloquia Peripatetica* (Edinburgh: Edmonston & Douglas, 1870), 105.

The trilemma was given a fuller, more memorable formulation in a speech by C. S Lewis in 1942 on the BBC, and later published in *Mere Christianity*.[3]

Among the points being made by both Duncan and Lewis is that it is impossible to call Jesus a good man (let alone, divine) if He either willfully or involuntarily deceived His listeners on core beliefs. And, short of distrusting the biblical records, we have no choice but to insist that the biblical testimony as to what Jesus believed about hell is very clear.

Edward Donnelly, after describing some "crude, inaccurate and unbiblical" caricatures of the sufferings of hell, goes on to insist:

> Yet we must face up to the horror of hell's sufferings, for the Bible reveals them to us, vividly and at length. The Lord Jesus himself describes hell in detail and we are certainly not more sensitive or more tender of the sensibilities of God's people than he was. To claim that we are too refined and humane to consider such things would be to criticize our Saviour. He spoke graphically about what hell will be like and we should think about his words as seriously as we can.[4]

Do you Believe in Hell?

In today's secular culture, *hell* (like *God* and *Jesus*) are mere swear words—expletives people utter for emphasis and with no thought whatsoever of what the words actually mean and certainly no expectation that the words convey an objective reality. Recent polling in the United States suggests that most evangelicals believe in hell's objective existence. In response to the statement, "Hell is a real place where certain people will be punished forever," 86% of those who called themselves evangelical agreed. Less certain in the poll, however, was the reason why certain people will be there. In response to the statement, "Even the smallest sin deserves eternal damnation," only 38% of evangelicals strongly agreed, with another 10% agreeing "somewhat." In other words, the majority of evangelicals believe that hell is only for those who commit a great sin of some kind.[5]

---

3. C. S. Lewis, *Mere Christianity* (San Francisco: Harper One, 2009), 53–54.

4. Edward Donnelly, *Biblical Teaching on the Doctrines of Heaven and Hell* (Edinburgh: The Banner of Truth, 2001), 33.

5. Lifeway Research and Ligonier Ministries. "The State of Theology," https://thestateoftheology.com/

However, both Jesus and the apostles rejoice—yes, that is the right word—in God's holy and righteous character, and insist that all sin, however small or insignificant in our estimation, is offensive to Him. God cannot condone sin or leave it unpunished. God demands *satisfaction*—a term that Anselm of Canterbury, and later, the Reformation and subsequent seventeenth-century confessions, adopted as accurately depicting what results from the atoning work of Christ. Thus, the *Westminster Confession of Faith* insists that Jesus died "to *satisfy* divine justice" (8.5).

Consequently, Jesus and the apostles (reflecting as they do Old Testament prophets and psalmists) exult in the vindication of God's honor and justice, seeing His acts of divine judgement, temporal or eschatological, as assurances of God's immutability and dependability to govern by the rule of law.

Further, Jesus and the apostles speak of hell as a real place of conscious existence, warning unbelievers to flee from it while assuring believers that they will never experience it. Hell is a place of pain, comparable to that of burning, in which the unrighteous and unforgiving will realize 1) how repulsive was their way of life on earth; 2) how just their present exclusion from heaven is; 3) how utterly beyond all joy and happiness they now are; and 4) how fixed their current position is.

What those who are in hell know is that they have what they, in fact, have chosen—a life without God and without the happiness that it brings. They have reaped precisely what they have sown in this life and hell is a confirmation of what they so earnestly pursued on earth: no more, no less.

Those who affirm hell are today denigrated as insensitive masochists, lost in a world of hatred and intolerance, ridiculed like no other as purveyors of hate speech, and even ostracized as sad obscurantists of a medieval worldview long since consigned to the dustbin of the past. Today, all views are true—a nonsensical statement believed by a vast majority of people as a way of ignoring vital elements of difficulty. Christianity stubbornly claims that this is decidedly not so: if Jesus is wrong about hell, or His own identity, or His insistence that no other way to heaven exists apart from faith in Him (see, John 1:14 for example), then He cannot be respected at all, let alone believed. Swimming against the stream of late modernity can be difficult, as it discredits any who don't agree with it. For instance, one notes the current rage against Jonathan Edwards's attempts to convey hell in graphic (yet, biblically informed) terms as disgusting and obscene, as he did in his sermon, *Sinners in the Hands of an Angry God.*

It is important, therefore, to ask, what does the Bible teach about hell? But in doing so, we face a terrible dilemma. If we really believe in hell, and that it is not an empty idea, how can we talk about it without a measure of pain and grief? The answer, of course, is that we cannot. When Robert Murray M'Cheyne met his dearest friend, Andrew Bonar, one Monday and inquired what Bonar had preached on the previous day, he replied, "Hell." And M'Cheyne responded, "And did you preach on it with tears?"[6]

What Jesus Teaches Us about Hell

Limiting ourselves to the teaching of Jesus exposes the Gordian knot of this position: can I still truly worship Him if I don't accept His words about hell?

Jesus's Testimony to the Reality of Eternal Punishment

The reality of punishment provides the background and explains the significance of why Jesus came in the first place. The Father loved this fallen world so much that "he gave his only begotten Son, that whosoever believes in him should not perish but have everlasting life" (John 3:16). Without the redemptive work of Christ, there is the certainty of "perishing" (v. 16), of "condemnation" (v. 18), and "the wrath of God" (v. 36). Apart from faith in Christ, there is the certainty of judgment.

Jesus Consistently Depicts Two Ways and Two Destinies

The parable of the weeds (Matt. 13:24–30) depicts the wheat as being harvested but the weeds as bound "in bundles to burn them" (v. 30). The parable of the net (Matt. 13:47–50) depicts a trailing net gathering both "good" and "bad" fish. The good are placed in containers but the "wicked" are said to be thrown away, just as at the end of the age the "evil" will be thrown into the "furnace of fire," where there will be "wailing and gnashing of teeth" (vv. 48, 50). The parable of the

---

6. Sinclair Ferguson, "Pastoral Theology: The Preacher and Hell," in *Hell Under Fire: Modern Scholarship Reinvents Eternal Punishment,* ed. Christopher Morgan and Andrew Peterson (Grand Rapids: Zondervan, 2004), 234.

foolish virgins (Matt. 25:1–13) speaks of "wise" virgins who are ready and enter into the marriage celebration along with the bridegroom, but the "foolish virgins" are shut out of the wedding (v. 10). And in the depiction of the final judgment in Matthew 25:31–46, Jesus paints a scene where a king is separating sheep from goats, the former on His right and the latter on His left, adding, "Then shall he say also unto them on the left hand, Depart from me, ye cursed, into everlasting fire, prepared for the devil and his angels" (v. 41).

Jesus tells a parable of a rich man (tradition calls him "Dives" from the Latin word for "rich man" in the Latin Vulgate) who ends up in Hades while Lazarus, following his death, goes to "Abraham's bosom" (Luke 16:19–31). Jesus marveled at the faith of the Gentile centurion who asked that his servant be healed. Responding, Jesus warned that "the sons of the kingdom [those who were ancestral descendants of Abraham, but did not believe in Jesus], will be cast out into the outer darkness. In that place there will be weeping and gnashing of teeth" (Matt. 8:12). In urging His disciples to persevere in the faith and not to presume their salvation by wanton neglect of mortification and self-denial, He warned that those who did not engage in killing ongoing sin were in danger of being "cast into hell fire, where their worm dieth not, and the fire is not quenched" (Mark 9:47–48). In this last reference, Jesus is citing Isaiah 66:24, the very last verse of Isaiah. The final chapter of Isaiah provides a magnificent picture of the new heaven and new earth—the future residence of the people of God and the final peroration of God's redemptive purpose. It is picked up again and expanded upon in the closing two chapters of the Bible (Rev. 21:22).[7] The *worm* and *fire* is a reference to the corpses left rotting and unburied after a battle—a disgrace in biblical times. To refuse burial was a horrendous humiliation. Fires broke out and were eventually extinguished. Maggots finished off the process of decay, but these, too, eventually would die. But in Hades, the fire is *never* extinguished, and the worm *never dies*. So appalled were the Jews by this ending of Isaiah that it was never read in public!

---

7. See my book, *Heaven on Earth: What the Bible Teaches about Life to Come* (Geanies House, Fearn: Christian Focus Publications, 2018), 81–94.

Objections

If the testimony of the Gospels is clear as to what Jesus said and believed about hell, why do some still refuse to accept it? One answer, and one that will not detain us here, is a belief in some form of limited inerrancy of Scripture. The objection suggests that we simply cannot be sure what Jesus said about many things—hell, or anything else, for that matter. We are lost in Lessing's "ugly ditch of history," which is skeptical of what can be known of the past. But this is a catch-22 argument that forces us to be skeptical of *anything* Jesus said (and for that matter His very existence) and not just of the particulars about His statements on hell.

Narrowing the issue, and assuming Scripture's accuracy (infallibility and inerrancy), what are the arguments against belief in hell?

The first objection arises due to *genre*. In short, there is a question as to how we interpret *parables*. It raises a question about symbolic language in Scripture. There is the use of simile and metaphor, of parable and the apocalyptic genre. These genres depict matters using vivid colors and exaggerated contours. So the question arises, do we then not need to be careful about interpreting such things *literally*?

The question is a tricky one because behind it lies the assumption that, since the matter is depicted in poetry and metaphor, there is no *reality* behind it. But that would be a categorical mistake. In one important sense, all Scripture should be interpreted *literally*—that is to say, "mindful of the type of literature that is being employed." Thus, parables should be interpreted in a way mindful of the particular nuance of parabolic literature. It is the same case with other genres, like poetry, narrative, prose, law, prophecy, and history.[8] R. C. Sproul explains this in a helpful manner:

> Whenever I enter into discussions about the doctrine of hell, people ask, "R. C., do you believe that the New Testament portrait of hell is to be interpreted literally?" When we look at some of the statements that are made about hell in the New Testament, we see that it is described in various ways—as a place of torment, as a pit or an abyss, as a place of eternal fire, and as a place of outer darkness. When people ask me whether these images of hell are to be interpreted literally, I usually respond

---

8. See Derek Thomas, *The Bible: God's Inerrant Word* (Edinburgh: Banner of Truth, 2018), 93–100.

by saying, "No, I don't interpret those images literally," and people respond with a sigh of relief.

One of the reasons classical orthodox theology has tended not to interpret these images literally is because if you do, you have a very difficult time making them agree with one another. If hell is a place of burning fire on the one hand and a place of outer darkness on the other hand, that's difficult to reconcile, because usually where there's fire there's light. You can't have fire in a total darkness. So there's a collision of images here.

Dr. Sproul then explains the function of symbols in the New Testament:

The function of figurative language in Scripture is to demonstrate a likeness to a reality. The symbol is not the reality itself. The symbol points beyond itself to something else. The question is whether the reality to which the symbol points is less intense than what is indicated by the symbol. The assumption is that there is always more to the reality than what is indicated by the symbol, which makes me think that, instead of taking comfort that these images in the New Testament may indeed be symbolic, we should be worrying that the reality toward which these symbols point is more ghastly than the symbols. I once heard a theologian say that a sinner in hell would do anything he could and give anything he had to be in a lake of fire rather than be where he actually is. So even if we don't know exactly what hell is, how hell operates, and what it is really like, all of the imagery our Lord uses suggests that it is a place we don't want to go. It is a place of unspeakable pain and torment.[9]

Conditionalism

Another objection to hell is a view known as *conditionalism*, or annihilationism. This is the view that the lost will eventually be annihilated. They will cease to exist.

Some annihilationists believe that this occurs immediately after death, or subsequent to a period of suffering on the day of judgment. Both Jehovah's Witnesses and Seventh Day Adventists hold to this view (with some differences). Jehovah's Witnesses believe that annihilation takes place immediately after death. Seventh Day Adventists

---

9. R. C. Sproul, *Unseen Realities: Heaven, Hell, Angels and Demons* (Geanies House, Scotland; Lake Mary, Fla.: Christian Focus Publications; Ligonier Ministries, 2011), 53–54.

believe that the wicked will be punished in the lake of fire before being destroyed.[10] According to this view, biblical texts that suggest *endless* punishment refer to the destructive forces that are employed and the results of this punishment as being eternal, and not that the wicked specifically *experience conscious torment* throughout eternity.[11]

Conditionalism arose early in the first century and in the second century. Ignatius of Antioch (c. AD 35/50–98/117), Justin Martyr (AD 100–165), Irenaeus (AD 130–202) and Arnobius of Sicca (also known as Arnobius the Elder [died c. 330]) all believed in conditionalism. Arnobius's words are often cited by adherents of this view:

> Your interests are in jeopardy, the salvation, I mean of your souls; and unless you give yourselves to seek to know the Supreme God, a cruel death awaits you when freed from the bonds of Body, *not bringing sudden annihilation*, but destroying by the bitterness of its grievous and long-protracted punishment.[12]

The idea of eternal conscious punishment emerges especially in Atheagoras of Athens (AD 133–190) in his *The Resurrection of the Dead* and Tertullian (AD 160–220), Hippolytus (AD 170–235), Cypriot (c. AD 200–258), Ambrose (AD 337–397), Chrysostom (AD 347–407), Jerome (AD 347–420), and Augustine (AD 354–450). In recent times, some well known evangelical scholars have advanced the notion of conditional immortality, including John Wenham, Philip Edgecombe Hughes, and John Stott.[13]

---

10. See A. A. Hoekema, *The Bible and the Future* (Exeter: Paternoster Press, 1978), 266.

11. See, for example, Clark Pinnock's view in *Four Views on Hell*, ed. Stanley N. Gundry (Grand Rapids: Zondervan, 1996), 135–66.

12. *Against the Heathen*, Book II, #61. Scholars continue to debate whether this statement is an affirmation of annihilationism.

13. John Wenham, *The Goodness of God* (Downers Grove, Ill.: InterVarsity Press, 1974); Philip Edgecombe Hughes, *The True Image: The Origin and Destiny of Man in Christ* (Grand Rapids: Eerdmans, 1989); John R. W. Stott's conversation with David Edwards in *Essentials: A Liberal-Evangelical Dialogue* (Downers Grove, Ill.: InterVarsity Press, 1988). For rebuttals of these works, see D. A. Carson, *The Gagging of God: Christianity Confronts Pluralism* (Grand Rapids: Zondervan, 1996), 515–36, and J. I. Packer, *Evangelical Affirmations* (Grand Rapids: Zondervan Academic, 1990), 107–48; Christopher W. Morgan and Robert A. Peterson, eds., *Hell Under Fire: Modern Scholarship Reinvents Eternal Punishment* (Grand Rapids: Zondervan, 2004), 30–31, 196–97, 209, 217, 220, 229.

Summarizing the arguments against annihilationism, four points should be made:

1. Annihilationists argue that too much has been made of the suffering of Dives in the parable of the rich man and Lazarus, insisting (correctly) that this is a portrayal of the intermediate state and not the final state. The allegation that this passage has often been misunderstood is fair enough, but it cannot be denied that there are New Testament passages that clearly extend *beyond* the intermediate state and imply a conscious suffering subsequent to the last judgment. Romans 2:5–16 depicts the final judgment according to a meticulous consideration of all that we have done or failed to do. Paul adds that there will be "tribulation and anguish, upon every soul of man that doeth evil" (Rom. 2:9). And more pertinent to our consideration in this chapter, Jesus speaks of an existence subsequent to the last judgment when he says in Matthew 8: "And I say unto you, That many shall come from the east and west, and shall sit down with Abraham, and Isaac, and Jacob, in the kingdom of heaven. But the children of the kingdom shall be cast out into outer darkness: there shall be weeping and gnashing of teeth" (11–12). The conscious experience of desolation and torment associated with Jesus's metaphors depicts conscious endurance of suffering in the final state of existence.

2. Annihilationists argue that insufficient care has been applied to the meaning of the words "eternal," "destruction," and "death" in passages alluding to the final state. Specifically, they argue that nouns that occur in conjunction with an "eternal" do not specify an action that is endless, but a result that is enduring. For example, in Mark 3:29, "eternal sin" (ESV) is not sin that goes on and on, but sin that has eternal consequences. And by parity of reasoning, the idea of "endless punishment" is not a reference to punishment that will be experienced for eternity but one (annihilation) whose consequences cannot be undone. The problem with this line of reasoning is that the exact same words are used in connection with "eternal life" where the reasoning is reversed.

3. Annihilationists argue that the New Testament terminology for the future state of the wicked includes language which signifies actual annihilation. Thus, "death" implies cessation.

Folk cease to exist in this dimension. Similarly, the "second death" must also imply a form of annihilation, a ceasing to be. The argument pursues the same reasoning what we saw in number 2 above, that traditionalists over-emphasize the adjective "eternal," and thereby miss the force of the *noun* "death." In this view, it is argued that death is an eternal cessation of existence and not an eternal consciousness. However, death in Scripture is the opposite of life-in-communion, whether with man or with God; it is not the opposite of existence *per se*. Indeed, it implies a certain kind of existence—"we know we have passed from death to life because we love the brethren" (1 John. 3:14). Or take Jesus's use of the metaphor of the undying worm in Mark 9:47–48. As we saw earlier, the background of this image lies in the closing verses of Isaiah 66. It is the picture of maggots eating away at rotting flesh. While traditional exegesis assumes that everlasting torment is in view, annihilationists argue that destruction is in view. If the annihilationists are correct, would it not be exegetically significant to say that the worms do not die nor are the fires quenched if the victims they consume no longer exist? When metaphors are stretched beyond their intended limit, they do not make the annihilationists' case.

4. Annihilationists argue that passages like Ephesians 1:9–10 and Colossians 1:18–20 (passages which speak of all things being reconciled or headed up in Christ), and 1 Corinthians 15:28 (announcing that God will be all in all), suggest that there will be no lost souls on God's *left* hand. Traditionalists, on the other hand, have viewed the ultimate eschatological existence to be permanently bifurcated. This was what Augustine pictured in his description, which was the death blow to universalism[14] in the early church: "After the resurrection, when general judgment hath been made and finished, then shall the two kingdoms have their accomplishment; the one, that is, the kingdom of Christ, the other, the kingdom of the devil; the one of the good, and the other of the evil."[15]

---

14. For an analysis of universalism, historically and theologically, see J. I. Packer, "Universalism: Will Everyone Ultimately be Saved?" in *Hell Under Fire*, 170–94.

15. Augustine, *Enchiridion* 111, in *A Select Library of the Nicene and Post-Nicene Fathers of the Christian Church, Volume III*, ed. Philip Schaff (Grand Rapids: Eerdmans, 1980), 273.

In part, the annihilationists' argument for the cessation of existence answers the very real dilemma forced upon the traditionalist point of view, the eternal conscious existence of suffering. How will the righteous rejoice in the knowledge of the eternal conscious suffering of others (some whom they have known and loved)? The annihilationists' answer is *because they no longer exist*. And there is an understandable, even in part, desirable, closure to this argument.

How will the righteous rejoice in the knowledge of the eternal suffering of others? The answer must surely be that in that final, righteous condition, the judgment of the lost will be viewed as the right thing. For God not to judge would be destructive of all serious and meaningful morality and its consequent accountability.

The Concept of Hell

In conclusion, then, how should we view hell *as Jesus perceived and proclaimed it?* Four thoughts seem pertinent:

1. The symbolic use of apocalyptic terms such as worm, fire, darkness, weeping, grinding teeth, destruction, and torment suggest a negative relationship toward God and a consequent deprivation of all good—good, in the sense of that which we would view as valuable, pleasant, fulfilling, peace-inducing, and worthwhile. The displacement of hell is spatial and temporal (for all future life will be such as a consequence of createdness), but the principal idea is relational separation from God's favor. Hell is not so much God's *absence* but His "presence in wrath," forever conscious of His divine rejection, and therefore never able to come to peace of mind and soul and being. The key thought is deprivation. Those in hell know what they have lost and why they have lost it; and they deeply regret it.

2. The lost sentence themselves to eternal destruction in hell this side of death, by a volitional, unrepentant unwillingness to yield to the revelation of God in creation, providence, and for some (not all), special revelation. No one in hell is saying, "I don't know why I am here." In that respect, hell is God's final display of respect for human choices. In the sovereign, pre-determining choices of God, violence is never pressed upon the will of the creature.

3. Tertullian, Aquinas, and Jonathan Edwards's suggestion that contemplation of the torment of the damned will increase heaven's joy for the righteous seems to go beyond what Revelation 16:5–7 and 19:1–3 suggest. Nevertheless, saints will eternally rejoice that God is just and that justice will be done.[16]

4. Hell is an appalling prospect because it will never end. The fire is everlasting; the destruction has no endpoint. "The smoke of their torment ascends forever and ever" (Rev. 14:11). "They will be tormented day and night forever and ever" (Rev. 20:10). As Donnelly puts it, "The ultimate horror of hell is its everlastingness."[17]

We began by asking what Jesus's view of hell is. And we can answer this by saying that Jesus viewed hell as a destiny. It is the future human existence of all who oppose God here and now. It is a conscious, unending experience of dissolution and despair, a non-fulfilling sense of incompleteness and banishment where nothing satisfies their existence. It is a place of punishment, separation from God's favor and all that is good. It is unending. That is what Jesus taught and that is what we must accept as truth if we are to call Him Lord and Savior.

Practical Conclusions for Believers

We dare not conclude without asking what all this means for those of us who are God's people, right here, right now. Several things spring to the surface:

1. We should have a sense of urgency about evangelism and the Christian's call to make disciples. People all around us are heading off the cliff like an army of ants marching in formation, heedless of everything but themselves. One of the pernicious effects of universalism is the utter callousness it produces in us so that we neglect to warn our neighbor. If everyone is going

---

16. For example, see Tertullian *De Spectaculus* xxx; Thomas Aquinas, *Summa Theologiae*, Q. 94, "The relations of the saints toward the damned"; Jonathan Edwards, "The End of the Wicked Contemplated," in *The Wrath of Almighty God* (Morgan, Pa.: Soli Deo Gloria Publications, 1996), 375; and "The Justice of God in the Damnation of Sinners," in *The Works of Jonathan Edwards*, Vol. 1 (Carlisle, Pa.: Banner of Truth, 1998).

17. Edward Donnelly, *Biblical Teaching on the Doctrines of Heaven and Hell* (Edinburgh: Banner of Truth, 2001), 42.

to be saved, one way or another, why should I not spare myself the embarrassment and hard work of evangelism? But no one really wants to believe that Adolph Hitler and Joseph Stalin are in the same place as Jonathan Edwards. Every fiber of our being cries out that this would be entirely unfair and unjust. R. L. Dabney made the point very clear: "Can we contemplate the exposure of our friends, neighbors, and children to a fate so terrible, and feel so little sensibility and make efforts so few and weak for their deliverance? How can our unbelieving friends be made to credit the sincerity of our convictions? Here is the best argument of Satan for their skepticism."[18]

2. We should have a sense of seriousness about the Christian life and its responsibilities. The knowledge that hell exists for the wicked should make us serious about what Jesus asks us to do for Him. We are not suggesting gloom and morbidity. Nor are we suggesting anything like the current caricature against Christians (Reformed and Puritan-loving Christians in particular) that they live in perpetual fear that something might make them happy. No! Christians should be the happiest and most joyful people on earth. But it is tinged with a seriousness that here we have no continuing city and the time is short to ensure that we and our loved ones get to the lasting city. "Rivers of waters run down mine eyes, because they keep not thy law," the psalmist said (Ps. 119:136). How many tears have we shed for the lost?

3. We should trust in the sovereign purposes of God. Why are some saved and others are not? The ultimate answer lies in the mysterious truths of election and reprobation. It lies in the statements of Romans 9 about God's love of Jacob and hatred of Esau (Rom. 9:13). But these truths also include a compatiblist understanding of the relationship between sovereignty and human responsibility, implying that we have a charge to make the gospel known—and, that when this is done, we must trust God's purposes. We may find the concept of hell emotionally unbearable, but it lies within God's purposes.

4. We must have joy in the gospel. A clear understanding of the biblical doctrine of hell should make us grateful for the gospel as nothing else does. That hell exists, and that we will never

---

18. Robert L. Dabney, *Systematic Theology* (Carlisle, Pa.: Banner of Truth, 1985), 861–62.

experience it, is a joy unspeakable and full of glory. We have been delivered from hell by the sacrifice of Jesus as our substitute and sin-bearer. By His death, we have been spared hell. Because He suffered hell on the cross, His words of anguish, "My God, my God, why hast thou forsaken me?" become our salvation. God forsook Him that we might never be forsaken. The Father did not spare Him (Rom. 8:32), though He spared us. What wondrous love is this!

HISTORICAL STUDIES

CHAPTER 8

The Beauty and Glory of the Puritan Millennium

Greg A. Salazar

The last paragraph of the Westminster Confession of Faith (33.3) ends with a distinct but decidedly ambiguous statement on the nature of the coming of Christ and the end of this age:

> As Christ would have us to be certainly persuaded that there shall be a day of judgment, both to deter all men from sin; and for the greater consolation of the godly in their adversity: so will he have that day unknown to men, that they may shake off all carnal security, and be always watchful, because they know not at what hour the Lord will come; and may be ever prepared to say, Come Lord Jesus, come quickly, Amen.

Until recently, the topic of the Puritan doctrine of the last times has been a relatively neglected subject. Over the past several decades, a number of important studies have shed significant light on this important topic.[1] The most important of these studies was Crawford

---

1. Crawford Gribben, *The Puritan Millennium: Literature and Theology 1550–1682* (Dublin: Four Courts Press, 2000; rev. ed., Colorado Springs, Colo.: Paternoster, 2008). Unless stated, all quotes are from the revised edition. Crawford Gribben, "'Passionate Desires, and Confident Hopes': Puritan Millenarianism and Anglo-Scottish Union, 1560–1644," *Reformation & Renaissance Review* 4 (2002): 241–58; Jeffrey K. Jue, *Heaven upon Earth: Joseph Mede (1586–1638) and the Legacy of Millenarianism* (Dordrecht, Netherlands: Springer, 2006); Jeffrey K. Jue, "Puritan Millenarianism in Old and New England," in *The Cambridge Companion to Puritanism,* ed. John Coffey and Paul C. H. Lim (Cambridge: Cambridge University Press, 2008), 259–76; Anthony Milton, *Catholic and Reformed: The Roman and Protestant Churches in English Protestant Thought, 1600–1640* (Cambridge: Cambridge University Press, 1995); Mary Morrisey, "Elect Nations and Prophetic Preaching: Types and Examples in Lori Anne Ferrrell and Peter McCullouch, "The Paul's Cross Jeremiad," in *The English Sermon Revised: Religion, Literature and History 1600–1750* (Manchester: Manchester University Press, 2000), 43–58; Richard Thomas Bell, "The Minister, the Millenarian, and the Madman: The Puritan Lives of William Sedgwick, ca. 1609–1664," *Huntington*

Gribben's seminal work, which demonstrated that there was a spectrum of views of the last days among Puritans, which range from more radical to conservative estimations of the time and manner of Christ's return.[2] This essay will build on recent work, and especially Gribben's contribution, by examining Puritan formulations of the doctrine of the last times during the 1640s in the Westminster Standards. In particular, it will examine the specific content of these formulations and how the context of the 1640s shaped the motivations that underpinned the Puritans' crafting of these doctrines. An unwavering commitment to ground their doctrinal views in Scripture was at the heart of the Puritan movement. Thus, it will be argued that the Westminster Standards, and particularly the Confession of Faith, are a monument to the reality that in the midst of the millenarianism of the 1640s, the Westminster divines were keen not to push beyond the bounds of Scripture in their public confessional documents.[3] For the Puritans intentionally not only avoided the radical millenarianism being circulated during the 1640s but also deliberately crafted doctrinal statements that could be subscribed to by many. Although previous scholarly studies have presented an accurate recounting of the historical events and theological positions, almost none of them

---

Library Quarterly 81 (2018): 29–61; Joel R. Beeke and Mark Jones, *A Puritan Theology: Doctrine for Life* (Grand Rapids: Reformation Heritage Books, 2012), 773–818; For older studies, see Iain Murray, *The Puritan Hope: A Study in Revival and the Interpretation of Prophecy* (Edinburgh: Banner of Truth, 1971); Peter Toon, ed., *Puritans, the Millennium, and the Future of Israel* (Cambridge: James Clarke, 1970); Bernard Capp, *The Fifth Monarchy Men: A Study in Seventeenth-Century Millenarianism* (London: Faber and Faber, 1972); William Lamont, *Godly Rule: Politics and Religion, 1603–60* (London: Macmillan, 1969); Christopher Hill, *The World Turned Upside Down: Radical Ideas during the English Revolution* (London: Temple Smith, 1972); Paul Christianson, *Reformers in Babylon: English Apocalyptic Visions from the Reformation to the Eve of the Civil War* (Toronto: University of Toronto Press, 1978); Katharine Firth, *The Apocalyptic Tradition in Reformation Britain, 1530–1645* (Oxford: Oxford University Press, 1979); Bryan Ball, *A Great Expectation: Eschatological Thought in English Protestantism to 1660* (Leiden: Brill, 1975). For excellent studies of the eschatology of the Continental Reformers, see Irena Backus, *Reformation Readings of the Apocalypse: Geneva, Zurich, and Wittenberg* (Oxford: Oxford University Press, 2000); Irena Backus, "The Church Fathers and the Canonicity of the Apocalypse in the Sixteenth Century: Erasmus, Frans Titelmans, and Theodore Beza," *Sixteenth Century Journal* 29 (1998): 651–66.

2. Gribben, *Puritan Millennium*. It should be acknowledged that this essay is largely indebted to Crawford Gribben's excellent work and (though to a lesser extent) the chapters on eschatology in Beeke and Jones's *Puritan Theology*.

3. Gribben, *Puritan Millennium*, 244.

attempted to draw out the implications and lessons the contemporary church could glean from this important study. Therefore, this essay will conclude by highlighting the significant experiential and practical applications that can be drawn from a study of Puritan millennialism in the 1640s.

Methodological Pitfalls and Assumptions in Studying Puritan Eschatology

Before outlining the Puritans' various eschatological positions in their historical context, it is crucial to highlight the convictions that underpin this historical analysis of Puritan millennial views. First, as Richard Muller explains, to understand Puritan millennial views, one must understand the historical context in which these views were forged.[4] Theological positions are never formulated in a vacuum, and, as Crawford Gribben has argued, this was a period "of eschatological explosion."[5] The theological debates over Puritan millennialism were shaped by the turmoil of the English Civil War and the explosion of religious radicalism in the 1640s.

This essay also seeks to avoid the pitfalls of both the older secular and older confessional historiography. Peter Lake has argued that prior to Patrick Collinson's seminal study, *The Elizabethan Puritan Movement*, there were at least two distinct schools of historians of Puritanism in general and Puritan millennialism in particular. On the one hand, there were "secular" historians—most notably Christopher Hill and Max Weber—who studied Puritanism as a vehicle to understanding "the grand narratives of modernity"—particularly the connections between the Protestant work ethic and the rise of capitalism and the promotion of their own political, intellectual, or cultural secular agendas.[6] Likewise, older studies of Puritan millenarianism by secular historians have tended to assume that millennialism (and millenarianism in particular) and radicalism go hand in hand.[7] As Jeff Jue has argued, secular "historians argued that millenarianism provided a divine apocalyptic motivation for oppressed and disenfranchised

---

4. Richard Muller, *The Study of Theology* (Grand Rapids: Zondervan, 1991), xi.

5. Gribben, *Puritan Millennium*, 21.

6. Peter Lake, "The Historiography of Puritanism," in *The Cambridge Companion to Puritanism*, ed. John Coffey and Paul C. H. Lim (Cambridge: Cambridge University Press, 2008), 348–49.

7. Jue, "Puritan Millenarianism in Old and New England," 259.

Puritans in their struggle for social, political and economic reforms."
Since they "were less concerned about specific theological definitions
and exegetical details," these historians "employed a sociological
definition of millenarianism, which frequently associated millenarianism with revolution" by arguing that the Puritans believed that
their "revolt was justified" since they sought "to replace all ungodly
monarchic rule with the millennial reign of Jesus Christ."[8] A major
weakness of this approach was the way in which these historians'
lack of theological understanding distorted their understanding of
the motivations that underpinned Puritan millenarianism.[9]

On the other hand, at the other end of the spectrum are older
"denominational" historians who viewed themselves as part of the
continuing "living tradition" of Puritanism and primarily focused on
Puritan theology and spirituality in their works.[10] Many of these historians downplayed the diversity within Puritanism and portrayed
Puritanism as a largely "homogeneous" movement.[11] Moreover, Gribben has pointed out that a significant theme in this historiography is
how historians and theologians "cited the Westminster Confession in
support of their preferred eschatology."[12] For example, while Robert
Clouse has argued that the Westminster Confession of Faith supported
amillennialism, LeRoy Froom believed it supported premillennialism,
and James Jong used the Confession to argue for postmillennialism.[13]

These examples hint that there is a deeply flawed methodological
assumption in this approach. For the term *eschatology* was not used
until the nineteenth century, and these categories of millennialism
are "largely constructed by more recent eschatological enquiry, [and]
cannot be used as uncomplicated heuristic tools to explicate puritan

---

8. Jue, "Puritan Millenarianism in Old and New England," 259–60.

9. For a similar observation, see Gribben, *Puritan Millennium*, 7.

10. Lake, "Historiography of Puritanism," 349.

11. Gribben, *Puritan Millennium*, 238.

12. Gribben, *Puritan Millennium*, 8.

13. R. G. Clouse, "The Rebirth of Millenarianism," in *Puritans, the Millennium,
and the Future of Israel*, ed. Peter Toon (Cambridge: James Clarke, 1970), 60; L. E.
Froom, *The Prophetic Faith of Our Fathers: The Historical Development of Prophetic Inter-
pretation* (Washington: Review and Herald, 1948), 2:553; James de Jong, *As the Waters
Cover the Sea: Millennial Expectations in the Rise of Anglo-American Missions 1640–1810*
(Kampen: Kok, 1970), 38n11; Gribben, *Puritan Millennium*, 8–9.

texts."[14] In short, the various Puritan views of the last things transcends the nineteenth-century terms and definitions and "is much less precise, much more ambiguous, than contemporary terminology allows."[15] For these were not the only three positions in this period nor do they clearly map the positions of the Puritans.[16] We are well cautioned to avoid the inaccuracy that results from imposing modern categories on historical subjects, for modern definitions of eschatology are unreliable for understanding the Puritans' doctrine of the millennium.[17]

Although older secular and confessional historians were in many ways polar opposites—pursuing different focuses and agendas—they integrated Puritanism with their own identity. For each school "sought to identify in Puritanism the origins of issues about which they cared deeply, issues integral to their own identity."[18] Indeed, they share the same epistemological starting points and assumptions. As Brad Gregory has argued, secular "reductionist explanations of religion share the epistemological structure of traditional confessional history. Just as confessional historians explore and evaluate based on their religious convictions, reductionist historians of religion explain and judge based on their unbelief. Both assume present-day convictions, whether theistic or atheistic, as their starting point."[19]

This essay attempts to avoid these errors and tries, as accurately as possible, to explain Puritan millennial views in the way Puritans would have understood them. A correct understanding of Puritan millennial views demands methodological rigor and must seek to avoid the pitfalls of both approaches. On the one hand, it must resist the biases of secular approaches to religion by acknowledging that millennialism "was not something puritans studied so much as something in which they believed themselves to be involved, for

---

14. Alan E. Lewis, "Eschatology," in *Encyclopedia of the Reformed Faith*, ed. Donald M. McKim (Edinburgh: St Andrews Press, 1992), 122; Gribben, *Puritan Millennium*, 239.

15. Gribben, *Puritan Millennium*, 239.

16. Gribben, *Puritan Millennium*, 239.

17. Gribben, *Puritan Millennium*, preface to the revised edition; Beeke and Jones, *Puritan Theology*, 774.

18. Lake, "Historiography of Puritanism," 349–50.

19. Brad Gregory, *Salvation at Stake: Christian Martyrdom in Early Modern Europe* (Cambridge, Mass.: Harvard University Press, 2001), 11.

the implications of their eschatology were not purely theoretical."[20] On the other hand, as confessionally committed historians (like me) study those figures and confessions that have shaped their own theological tradition, they must be careful not to curtail the evidence to fit their own predetermined modern categories.

Puritan Millennial Views before and at the Westminster Assembly

Puritan millennial views were developed from the beginning of the Puritan movement, while the early Puritans were in exile following the Counter-Reformation under Mary I. From 1553 to 1558, Henry VIII's daughter Mary I sought to reverse the reforms enacted during the previous decades of the English Reformation. As a result of her reforms, the deposed Roman Catholic bishops were restored, and she resorted to widespread persecution of hundreds of Protestants, thus earning her the nickname "Bloody Mary." She performed these executions publicly—going even as far as executing the three most significant Protestant leaders—Thomas Cranmer, Hugh Latimer, and Nicholas Ridley—by burning them at the stake in the middle of the town center in Oxford. In total, eight hundred Protestants fled England during this time, with many of the more prominent Protestants fleeing to Germany and Geneva because they had read the works of Continental Reformers and found a safe haven from the persecution.

The early Reformers' doctrine of the last things was of a conservative brand of Augustinianism that avoided projecting any specific kind of historicist interpretation on the current events.[21] The experience of exile within their newfound Reformed communities had a profound effect on Puritan eschatology. And it was ultimately during their flight to Geneva that Puritan eschatology was developed. Indeed, Puritans saw parallels between their experience of exile and the experiences of the saints in the books of Daniel and Revelation.[22] For example, "the preface to the first edition of the Geneva Bible (1560) described the exiles as a remnant that 'loves the coming of Christ Jesus our Lord.'"[23]

---

20. Gribben, *Puritan Millennium*, 13–14.
21. Beeke and Jones, *Puritan Theology*, 774.
22. Beeke and Jones, *Puritan Theology*, 776; Gribben, *Puritan Millennium*, 59.
23. *The Geneva Bible* (1560), sig.iiiv; Gribben, *Puritan Millennium*, 246.

There was a variety of eschatological views within the Puritan tradition, and some Puritans were sympathetic to a "historicist" interpretation of apocalyptic texts.[24] Some even traced continuities between the apocalyptic prophecies of Daniel and Revelation and their own experiences during the 1640s.[25] As Joel R. Beeke and Mark Jones have argued, for these Puritans, a historicist approach to these texts was not "vain speculation" or opposed to their commitment to "*sola Scriptura*." Instead, they believed it was precisely their commitment to *sola Scriptura* that compelled them to draw these conclusions.[26] Indeed, in Thomas Goodwin's son's preface to his father's work *An Exposition of the Revelation*, he said that his father's "assertions herein are no other than according to those measures the word of God has prescribed, he has fetched his proofs from the same magazine; and the evidence of his arguments is the more convincing, since it proceeds from that light which he beats out by comparing places of Scripture together." Moreover, to those who would "judge some of his notions to be too fine, and condemn his thoughts for taking too high a flight and leaping over the common bounds of knowledge; this may be pleaded in defence, that he has at least asserted nothing that contradicts a received truth, or which by any consequence may weaken the foundations of religion. Nay, he asserts nothing but what divine authority in Scripture does countenance."[27] Indeed, Goodwin and the Puritans were convinced that their conclusions were grounded on the solid foundation of the Word of God and sought by whatever means necessary to avoid going beyond the bounds of Scripture.

Underpinning the Puritans' historicist reading of the biblical texts was their belief that although "ongoing" new revelation had ceased with the completion of the New Testament canon, Scripture allowed for ongoing "mediated prophecy" of future events through the text of Scripture.[28] In his excellent study of this subject, Garnet Milne argues that "it is a belief in mediate prophecy, in which Scripture plays the central role, which explains why the cessation of immediate prophecy was not seen to nullify the availability of

---

24. Beeke and Jones, *Puritan Theology*, 774–75.

25. Beeke and Jones, *Puritan Theology*, 775.

26. Beeke and Jones, *Puritan Theology*, 774.

27. Thomas Goodwin Jr., preface to *An Exposition of the Revelation*, in *Works of Thomas Goodwin*, 12 vols. (Eureka, Calif.: Tanski, 1996), 3:xxviii.

28. Beeke and Jones, *Puritan Theology*, 775.

insight into the future for those who lived by the written Word of God."[29] In short, "mediate prophecy is not the revelation of new truth from God but the Spirit-enabled interpretation of biblical prophecies and application of those prophecies to unfolding history."[30]

Far from being fail-safe interpretations, it was expected that these predictions could (and indeed would) at times be fallible.[31] Moreover, Puritans viewed the appropriation of these Scriptures to the whole sphere in which they lived as a natural implication of their impetus to apply biblical doctrine to all of life. With the benefit of hindsight, we know that their interpretation and application of these apocalyptic texts was misguided. Nevertheless, we must keep in mind that it was not only the Marian exile but also the persecutions under William Laud and the experience of the English Civil War that led many Puritans to believe that they were living in the very last days of the world.[32] Along with his persecution of Puritans, Laud, with the support of Charles I, revised the Book of Common Prayer in 1637 in a distinctly Roman Catholic direction and then proceeded to try to impose it on Calvinist Scotland. This, of course, led to the Scottish revolution, when the Scottish-Presbyterians rebelled, with English Presbyterians eventually joining them. At the same time, Roman Catholics in Ireland joined forces with the monarchy and killed one hundred thousand Protestants. As Jeff Jue points out, "The Protestants' fears of popery and the Antichrist were confirmed and the king himself was thought to be allied with these demonic forces."[33]

It is no wonder that in the same year as these events, 1637, Richard Sibbes, in his *Spiritual Man's Aim*, boldly proclaimed, "There is but a little time before the day of judgement. Christ is at hand to judge the quick and the dead. The time between this and that is short…. We are fallen into the latter end of the world."[34] When we consider the utter turmoil that Sibbes and other Puritans experienced, it is not hard to understand why they believed these prophecies of final judgment

29. Garnet Howard Milne, *The Westminster Confession of Faith and the Cessation of Special Revelation* (Eugene, Ore.: Wipf and Stock, 2007), 210.

30. Beeke and Jones, *Puritan Theology*, 775.

31. Beeke and Jones, *Puritan Theology*, 775.

32. Beeke and Jones, *Puritan Theology*, 775.

33. Jue, "Puritan Millenarianism," 264.

34. Richard Sibbes, *The Spiritual Man's Aim*, in *The Works of Richard Sibbes*, 7 vols. (Edinburgh: Banner of Truth, 1983), 4:43.

were analogous to the events of this time. Indeed, this belief may have actually fueled a further justification of mediated revelation, since the end of days was a time when "knowledge shall increase."[35]

A historicist approach to apocalyptic texts also flourished in the following decade during the English Civil War of the 1640s, when significant political transitions took place as Charles I was defeated, captured, and beheaded and a republic was established with Oliver Cromwell as the Lord Protector of England. These events, combined with the dissolving of censorship of the press and the invention of the newspaper in the 1640s, led to a dramatic spike in works on millennialism.[36] It was in this context that on June 12, 1643, Parliament issued an ordinance summoning "an Assemblie of Learned and Godlie divines." This gathering, eventually known as the Westminster Assembly, was "for the settling of the Government and Litturgie of the Church of England" and "for the vindicating and clearing the doctrine…from false Aspersions and Interpretations."[37] Made up of approximately 150 members, the Assembly was convened on July 1, 1643, to refine orthodoxy in England following a decade of Laudian reform. Although it originally set out to revise the Thirty-Nine Articles, the Assembly met over 1,300 times from 1643 to 1653 and produced not only the Westminster Confession of Faith and Larger and Shorter Catechism but a Directory of Worship, a psalter, and various other documents related to the Assembly.[38] The Confession, in particular, was intended to be a biblical guide, demonstrated by the twenty-five hundred "proof texts" in this 12,000 word document.[39] It

---

35. Gribben, *Puritan Millennium*, 262.

36. Beeke and Jones, *Puritan Theology*, 776.

37. *The Minutes and Papers of the Westminster Assembly 1643–1652*, ed. Chad Van Dixhoorn, et. al. (5 vols., Oxford: Oxford University Press, 2012), 1:165, hereafter cited as *MPWA*. Van Dixhoorn's study of the minutes has replaced the older studies of the minutes: A. F. Mitchell, *The Westminster Assembly: Its History and Standards* (Philadelphia: Presbyterian Board of Publication, 1884); S. W. Carruthers, *The Everyday Work of the Westminster Assembly* (Philadelphia: Presbyterian Historical Society of America, 1943); and R. S. Paul, *The Assembly of the Lord: Politics and Religion in the Westminster Assembly and the "Grand Debate"* (Edinburgh: T&T Clark, 1985). For another recent study addressing the issue of ecclesiology at the Westminster Assembly, see Hunter Powell, *The Crisis of British Protestantism: Church Power in the Puritan Revolution, 1638–44* (Manchester: Manchester University Press, 2015).

38. *MPWA*, 1:1.

39. Chad Van Dixhoorn, *Confessing the Faith: A Reader's Guide to the Westminster Confession of Faith* (Edinburgh: Banner of Truth, 2014), xix, 179.

is no wonder that over the past three centuries, numerous Reformed and Presbyterian denominations have adopted these documents as their confessional and denominational standards, and many have argued that they represent the high point of Reformed orthodoxy in early modern England.

It is fascinating to explore the way in which Puritan millennial thought developed throughout the Assembly by analyzing particular sections of documents produced by it. For example, an examination of the instructions given in *The Directory for the Publick Worship of God* (1644) as to what ministers should pray for in the "Publick Prayer before the Sermon" is revealing. There, ministers are urged "to pray for the propagation of the gospel and kingdom of Christ to all nations, for the conversion of the Jews, the fullness of the Gentiles, the fall of Antichrist, and the hastening of the second coming of our Lord."[40]

These directions reveal that in 1644 there appears to have been an understanding that a number of events were linked with the coming of Christ—the proclamation of the gospel through the world, a mass conversion of Jews to Christianity, and the destruction of the Anti-christ (in this case, most likely, the papacy). Likewise, question 191 of the Westminster Larger Catechism proposes a similar eschatological view when it expounds what we are to understand when we pray "Thy kingdom come" in the Lord's Prayer. There we are instructed to

> pray, that the kingdom of sin and Satan may be destroyed, the gospel propagated throughout the world, the Jews called, the fullness of the Gentiles brought in; the church furnished with all gospel-officers and ordinances, purged from corruption, countenanced and maintained by the civil magistrate: that the ordinances of Christ may be purely dispensed, and made effectual to the converting of those that are yet in their sins, and the confirming, comforting, and building up of those that are already converted: that Christ would rule in our hearts here, and hasten the time of his second corning, and our reigning with him for ever: and that he would be pleased so to exercise the kingdom of his power in all the world, as may best conduce to these ends.[41]

---

40. The Directory for the Publick Worship of God, in *The Westminster Confession of Faith* (Glasgow: Free Presbyterian Publications, 1967), 377. Also see Murray, *Puritan Hope*, 44; Gribben, *Puritan Millennium*, 254.

41. The Larger Catechism, in *Westminster Confession of Faith*, 274–75.

Nevertheless, while there were features of these more historicist interpretations in the Directory and Larger Catechism, the Confession of Faith (33.3) presents a slightly less precise eschatological position by positing a more open-ended, rather than fixed, interpretation of the last day:

> As Christ would have us to be certainly persuaded that there shall be a day of judgment, both to deter all men from sin; and for the greater consolation of the godly in their adversity: so He will have that day unknown to men, that they may shake off all carnal security, and be always watchful, because they know not at what hour the Lord will come; and may be ever prepared to say, Come Lord Jesus, come quickly. Amen.[42]

Moreover, reflecting on these passages, Crawford Gribben has pointed out that the Assembly's "most extensive treatment of" eschatological issues "is linked to the Assembly's wider project, involving world evangelism and a last-days revival, proper ecclesiology, the theonomic rule of the 'godly prince,' and the eternal reign of the saints." In this way the Assembly's eschatological positions were an expression of its "comprehensive programme for reform."[43]

Reflecting on the Assembly's eschatological statements in their historical context allows us to note a number of interesting themes. First, given that Puritans were drawing from previous confessions (in particular, the Irish Articles), these statements are a reflection of Puritan eschatology in its most mature state.[44]

Second, in the midst of the radical millenarianism of the 1640s, Puritans took a self-consciously conservative and open-ended approach to eschatological issues. In 1640 the century-long practice of state-sanctioned censorship of the press was dissolved, and Parliament allowed effective freedom of expression—for the first time in English history. The result was a vast proliferation of sects—including Ranters, Anabaptists, Quakers, Diggers, Muggletonians—who took over local parish churches and established themselves wherever they could. The 1640s was thus a time when there was significant anxiety about heresy. Moreover, the Parliamentary army was a powerhouse of radical ideas, and its leaders soon entered into conflict with the

---

42. Gribben, *Puritan Millennium*, 255.
43. Gribben, *Puritan Millennium*, 255.
44. Gribben, *Puritan Millennium*, 255.

Presbyterians. These Independents were against any form of state-imposed church order or discipline. The apprehensions about heresy and fragmentation within Protestantism are a reflection of the myriad of issues facing Puritans, particularly as it pertains to eschatology. This context and these anxieties fueled the proliferation of millenarianism. The Westminster Assembly attempted to navigate this terrain by constructing a "careful [and] deliberate" eschatological position even though there were Assembly divines and other Puritans who appeared to have held more radical eschatological views.[45]

Third, eschatological conservatism appears to have been motivated, at least in part, by a desire to preserve theological consensus within a fairly diverse array of views on the millennium. Recent scholarship has explored the ways in which the Westminster Assembly divines sought to achieve theological consensus within a diversity of doctrinal positions on a variety of issues, including the imputation of the active obedience of Christ, hypothetical universalism, and the number and nature of the covenants, among other things.[46] One prominent issue that showcased the diversity of the Assembly and was directly linked to eschatology was ecclesiology. In particular, there was a cohort of English Congregationalists at Westminster. This group, known as the Dissenting Brethren, consisted of a number of well-known Puritan divines including Thomas Goodwin, Jeremiah Burroughs, Philip Nye, Sidrach Simpson, and William Bridge. In his study of the Dissenting Brethren, Hunter Powell has argued that these men were "a cohesive group, writing numerous pamphlets, manuscripts and confessions of faith together between 1635 and 1658," the most famous of which was the *Apologeticall Narration* (1644).[47] Gribben points out that the publication of *An Apologeticall Narration* indicates that the Dissenting Brethren believed that the Assembly's eschatological positions "were insufficiently exact" and "could be more closely refined."[48] It is no surprise, then, that when the Independents met for the Savoy Conference in 1658 they revised the Westminster

---

45. Gribben, *Puritan Millennium*, 253, 261–62.

46. The best book on this subject is Michael A. G. Haykin and Mark Jones, *Drawn into Controversie: Reformed Theological Diversity and Debates within Seventeenth-Century British Puritanism* (Göttingen: Vandenhoeck & Ruprecht, 2011).

47. Powell, *Crisis of British Protestantism*, 3.

48. Gribben, *Puritan Millennium*, 256.

Confession of Faith's statements on eschatology.[49] Gribben's insightful analysis is worth quoting at length:

> The Savoy Confession largely reiterates the Westminster's pronouncements on the intermediate state and the last judgment (Savoy 31–32, WCF 32–33). Its most innovative eschatological statements are included in chapter twenty-six, "Of the Church." Here, evidencing their distinctive patterns of ecclesiology, the Savoy divines expansively modified the Westminster Confession's formulae. They affirmed only the first paragraph of WCF 25, replacing subsequent paragraphs with a definition of the church which excluded baptized children from church membership and denied that the authority for the administration of ordinances or church government were given to the universal church, instead locating the foci of church authority in the local congregation (Savoy 26:2, contra WCF 25:2–3).[50]

This is one example of many indicating that while the Assembly's documents by their very nature give the impression of consensus among the divines, there were many within the group who would have preferred a more robust, refined, and detailed exposition of the specific issues related to the millennium. This, of course, reveals that the priority for the Assembly divines was consensus, compromise, and avoiding more radical and historicist eschatological expressions. Some have utilized the fact that the Confession is self-consciously conservative regarding the particulars of the millennium to argue that the Puritans were essentially articulating an amillennialist position.[51] But this fails to account for the Assembly being equally driven by a desire to achieve consensus as it was to avoid radicalism. In short, the Assembly members were attempting to craft a position that was general and open enough to support a variety of different eschatological positions while avoiding those theological points which were particularly controversial or perceived as potentially radical.[52] In this way, the Assembly's documents themselves defined the bounds of orthodoxy and therefore had a special level of flexibility.[53]

---

49. Gribben, *Puritan Millennium*, 257.

50. Gribben, *Puritan Millennium*, 257–58.

51. Louis Berkhof, *Systematic Theology* (Edinburgh: Banner of Truth, 1958), 708; Gribben, *Puritan Millennium*, 245.

52. For a similar argument, see Gribben, *Puritan Millennium*, 238, 244–45, 254.

53. Gribben, *Puritan Millennium*, 240.

Concluding Lessons for the Modern Church

There are a number of implications and lessons the modern church can glean from this study of Puritan eschatology during the 1640s. First, this study should give us an appreciation of the literal blood, sweat, and tears that went into crafting arguably the greatest confessional standards ever created. Often modern laypeople, or even pastors and theologians, fail to read the Standards within their political and ecclesiastical context. It is often overlooked or underappreciated that the Westminster Assembly took place in the context of the English Civil War. Once we grasp this, we realize that these were not armchair theologians, but men who were in the middle of a civil war—and a gruesome one at that. This was a war that completely changed the country—friends were divided against one another, the king was beheaded, and a completely new regime was implemented. This gives us insight into the pastoral sensitivity that must have driven these men. They truly understood that these issues were a matter of life and death because they were living at a time when they literally *became* a matter of life and death. And this, of course, emboldens us to continue to handle these issues with seriousness and to contend for the faith.

Second, a reflection on how the historical context shaped Puritan eschatology should caution us to be self-aware of how our current ecclesiastical, political, or social circumstances might shape our own theological positions. Indeed, a major theme of this study (and indeed the whole of church history) is how, despite our best efforts, theological positions are influenced by the context in which we live. Like many of the Puritans, it is all too easy for us to witness the turmoil both within and outside the church and either involuntarily (or even unintentionally) begin to project our own interpretation of events on Scripture.[54] This, of course, is not only a danger that exists as we read apocalyptic books but also as we exposit and apply any portion of the Bible.

Third, we can learn from the Puritans' desire to make Scripture their supreme authority in faith and practice. In their study of eschatology, Puritans did not shy away from investigating commentaries and other theological works of great divines. They were keen to

---

54. Beeke and Jones, *Puritan Theology*, 818.

make sure, however, that their views never went beyond and were firmly grounded in Scripture itself.[55]

Fourth, part of their strategy to achieve theological consensus was to distinguish between primary and secondary issues. When crafting the Assembly documents, some issues were nonnegotiable and some things were negotiable. Likewise, at times the modern church needs to better differentiate between primary and secondary theological issues. It seems that what motivated the Puritans was their desire, as far as it depended on them, to "live peaceably with all men" (Rom. 12:18). The Westminster divines modeled how Reformed theologians from different theological positions could work together and find unity by formulating doctrinal statements that could be subscribed by all parties.

Fifth, this study has challenged us to accept that even the most united ecclesiastical assemblies contain some measure of theological diversity. Before closely studying the Puritans, I assumed that these divines were a homogenous group of godly men and women who were wholly united, even in the minutest of theological points. When I began to discover divergences within the Puritan movement, my first reaction was to see this as a weakness. As time went on, however, I began to realize that these divergences were far from being a flaw with Puritanism; they were one of the movement's greatest strengths. These were men of deep theological conviction—willing to die for what they believed—who nevertheless were able to distinguish between primary and secondary issues and to love and work with those with whom they disagreed on lesser issues. There is much to learn here for our contemporary church as well. Too often in the Reformed community, we are defined by those secondary issues that divide us rather than the many features of our common confession and love and our unity with Christ, which holds us together. Thus, the beauty and glory of the Puritan millennium is that these Puritan divines rigorously maintained not only their diverse theological convictions but also genuine commitment to charity and consensus even in the midst of the political and ecclesiastical chaos that swirled around them.

---

55. Gribben, *Puritan Millennium*, 261–62.

CHAPTER 9

Jonathan Edwards: Surprised by the Beauty and Glory of God

Adriaan C. Neele

And as I was walking there, and looked up on the sky and clouds; there came into my mind, a sweet sense of the *glorious* majesty and grace of God, that I know not how to express.... The appearance of everything was altered: there seemed to be, as it were, a calm, sweet cast, appearance of divine *glory*, in almost everything.[1]

Thus said Jonathan Edwards (1703–1758) in his "Personal Narrative," noting, furthermore, "The sense I had of divine things, would often of a *sudden* as it were, kindle up a sweet burning in my heart; an ardor of my soul, that I know not how to express."[2] Edwards was surprised by the beauty and glory of God—not only at the time of his spiritual conversion in the spring of 1721, but throughout his life. As he was sitting alone under a tree or riding on a horse through the British colony of New England, he would experience times of communion with God. In 1737, for example, while walking in the woods, he had such a "view" of God's glory that for an hour he was "in a flood of tears, and weeping aloud." Such times of solitude and meditation were for Edwards occasions of renewal.[3]

The life of the probationer of New York, preacher of Northampton, missionary to the Mohican *Indians* at Stockbridge, and president of the College of New Jersey (now Princeton University), was not always in this frame. In fact, he writes,

---

1. *The Works of Jonathan Edwards* (New Haven: Yale University Press, 1957-) 16:793. Emphasis mine. Hereafter *WJE*. On Edwards's historical account of his own spiritual journey, see *WJE* 16:747–50.

2. *WJE* 16:793.

3. *WJE* 16:749 paraphrased.

From my childhood up, my mind had been wont to be full of objections against the doctrine of God's sovereignty, in choosing whom he would to eternal life, and rejecting whom he pleased; leaving them eternally to perish, and be everlastingly tormented in hell. It used to appear like a horrible doctrine to me.[4]

Furthermore, and in contrast to his "Personal Narrative" (a retrospective writing from a mature experience), Edwards's "Diary" recorded daily spiritual struggles as a young person in crisis. One finds entries such as, "Saturday, Dec. 29, [1722]. About sunset this day, dull and lifeless,"[5] and a year later, "Decayed...I find now and then, that abominable corruption which is directly contrary to what I read of eminent Christians,"[6] and just before leaving the Presbyterian congregation at New York in April 1723, he writes,

This week I found myself so far gone, that it seemed to me, that I should never recover more. Let God of his mercy return unto me, and no more leave me thus to sink and decay! I know, O Lord, that without thy help, I shall fall innumerable times, notwithstanding all my resolutions, how often so ever repeated.

When he mentions, "notwithstanding all my resolutions, how often so ever repeated," Edwards refers to his seventy "Resolutions" or "firm determinations," which "were neither pious hopes, romantic dreams, nor legalistic rules. They were instructions for life, maxims to be followed in all respects."[7] As he wrote,

Being sensible that I am unable to do anything without God's help, I do humbly entreat him by his grace to enable me to keep these Resolutions, so far as they are agreeable to his will, for Christ's sake. Remember to read over these Resolutions once a week.

Thus, Edwards's resolve and aim in life was: "I will do whatsoever I think to be most to God's glory," and "never to do any manner of thing, whether in soul or body, less or more, but what tends to the glory of God."[8]

---

4. *WJE* 16:791–92.

5. *WJE* 16:760.

6. *WJE* 16:761, "Wednesday, Jan. 9, at night. Decayed...."

7. *WJE* 16:741.

8. *WJE* 16:753, "1. Resolved, that I will do whatsoever I think to be most to God's glory, and my own good, profit and pleasure, in the whole of my duration,

The autobiographical nature of Edwards's "Resolutions," "Diary," and "Personal Narrative" shows a life that first objected to, yet became captured by, and eventually longed for, the glory and beauty of God. These reflections on divine glory and beauty in his private writings do not differ from his writings for the public, such as sermons and treatises, such as *A Faithful Narrative* (1736) and *A Treatise Concerning Religious Affections* (1746). Therefore, in what follows, I will explore *what* God's "glory" and "beauty" is for Edwards, and *why* he is surprised by it.

Edwards's Sense of the Glory of God

When Edwards reflects on God's glory and beauty, he does so as an acute observer of nature and Scripture. In fact, the preacher of New England sees in nature various types of the supernatural, the spiritual, God, and Christ. The type is the material creation by which God communicated to created minds the antitype, the spiritual reality. God reveals Himself to His creatures with the goal that He be glorified. Scripture, for Edwards, parallels this typology: a type was "some outward or sensible thing ordained of God under the Old Testament, to hold forth something of Christ in the New."[9]

Thus, Edwards distinguishes "divine glory" in *ad intra* and *ad extra*. The divine life "in itself" (*ad intra*) consists of love and happiness, and this glory finds its fullness in the Trinity. For Edwards, the second person of the Tri-unity is "the one in whom the Father's glory is made visible." Hence the "divine glory is supremely excellent, radiant in the fullness and joy of the love in which the divine life" exists.[10] Therefore, according to Edwards, "there are three things called by the name of *glory* in Scripture: excellency, goodness and happiness."[11]

---

without any consideration of the time, whether now, or never so many myriads of ages hence; 4. Resolved, never to do any manner of thing, whether in soul or body, less or more, but what tends to the glory of God; nor be, nor suffer it, if I can avoid it." See also "Resolution" 23 and 27, *WJE* 16:754–55.

9. Samuel Mather, *The Figures Or Types of the Old Testament: By which Christ and the Heavenly Things of the Gospel were preached and Shadowed to the People of God of Old*, 2nd ed. (London: Printed for Nath. Hillier, 1705), 52. Edwards consulted this work of Mather regularly.

10. Christina N. Larsen, "Glory," in Harry S. Stout, Kenneth P. Minkema, Adriaan C. Neele, *The Jonathan Edwards Encyclopedia* (Grand Rapids: Eerdmans, 2017), 252.

11. *WJE* 20:517. Emphasis mine.

This divine glory is not only manifested in itself, but this divine glory is also graciously communicated to His creatures (*ad extra*), since the end of creation is God's glory. As Edwards noted in "Miscellanies,"

> God loves his creatures so, that he really loves the being honored by them, as all try to be well thought of by those they love. Therefore, we are to seek the glory of God as that which is a thing really pleasing to him.[12]

That is not to say that His glory is dependent on the happiness of people, as Edwards writes, "Scripture make me think that God's glory is a good *independent* of the happiness of the creature."[13]

This is also not to suggest that God's sharing His glory with creation is aimed at making Him happier, as Edwards explains,

> for God to glorify himself, is, in his acts *ad extra*, to act worthy of himself, or to act excellently. Therefore God don't seek his own glory because it makes him the happier to be honored and highly thought of, but because he loves to see himself, his own excellencies and glories, appearing in his works, loves to see himself communicated.[14]

Creation, therefore, was primarily motivated by God's inclination to communicate Himself:

> His own glory was the ultimate [end], himself was his end; that is, himself communicated. The very phrase "the glory" seems naturally to signify [this]. Glory is a shining forth.... So that the glory of God is the shining forth of his perfections; and the world was created that they might shine forth, that is, that they might be communicated.[15]

Although, for Edwards, creation is a manifestation of divine glory, it is re-creation, or "redemption," in Edwards's words, in which God is most glorified. Thus, in Boston in the summer of 1731 he preached a sermon titled, *God Glorified in Man's Dependence* for the ministers of New England. It was based on 1 Corinthians 1:29–31: "That no flesh should glory in his presence. But of him are ye in Christ Jesus, who of

---

12. *WJE* 13:342.
13. *WJE* 13:358–59.
14. *WJE* 13:360–61.
15. *WJE* 13:360–61.

God is made unto us wisdom, and righteousness, and sanctification, and redemption: that, according as it is written, He that glorieth, let him glory in the Lord." In this sermon, the 28-year-old preacher develops themes he had been working on in his private notebooks and other sermons from the period.

Structured in a typical Edwardsean style of exegesis, doctrine, and application, the sermon unfolds the evangelical precept that human beings are so fallen that they are completely dependent on God for any and all spiritual good, especially salvation or redemption. If human beings are so dependent on God, Edwards reasons, then God redeems them out of "mere and arbitrary grace," which is to say, through the work of Christ and the presence of the Spirit. Thus, linking this Reformed understanding of humanity to the doctrine of the Trinity, Edwards contends that people "depend on Christ for redemption, on God for Christ, and on the Holy Spirit for the faith that unites them with Christ." This is sufficient reason for the redeemed *to glory in the Lord*, as all their good comes *from* God, *through* God's gift of Christ who justifies them; and so all their good is *in* God, who makes them morally excellent by the presence of the Holy Spirit. Thus Edwards infers that Arminian views on human nature, which deny humanity's complete dependence on God, contradict the very logic of the Trinity.[16] For Edwards, God's glory—this Trinitarian glory *ad intra*—is shared (*ad extra*) in creation with His creatures, and in redemption with the redeemed, who in return give Him all the glory, or, as the preacher expresses in the application of the sermon,

> [You have an] obligation to contemplate and acknowledge the glory and fullness of God. How unreasonable and ungrateful should we be, if we did not acknowledge that sufficiency and glory, that we do absolutely, immediately, and universally depend upon?

And so Edwards concludes,

> Let us be exhorted to exalt God alone, and ascribe to him all the glory of redemption…this doctrine should teach us to exalt God alone as by trust and reliance, so by praise. "Let him that glories glory in the Lord" [Jer. 9:24]. Hath any man hope that he is converted, and sanctified, and that his mind is endowed

---

16. *WJE* 17:196.

with true excellency and spiritual beauty, and his sins forgiven, and he received into God's favor, and exalted to the honor and blessedness of being his child, and heir of eternal life; let him give God all the glory.

Thus, the glory of God is the highest end of the work of redemption, a principle Edwards sees confirmed by the song of the angels at Christ's birth: "Glory to God in the highest, and on earth, peace and good will towards men" (Luke 2:14)

But Edwards has more to say about glory. Although Christ by His righteousness purchased for everyone perfect happiness (that is, He merited their capacity to be filled with happiness), the fact remains "that the saints, being of *various* capacities, may have *various* degrees of happiness," or various degrees of glory.[17] In fact, in the winter of 1739 Edwards notes in his private theological journal, "Miscellanies," that saints are "proportioning the degrees of glory." What does he mean by that? Although Christ's work is a finished work, Edwards argues,

> The saints are like so many vessels of different sizes cast into a sea of happiness, where every vessel is full: this is eternal life, for a man forever to have his capacity filled. But after all, 'tis left to God's sovereign pleasure, 'tis his prerogative, to determine the largeness of the vessel; and he may determine how he pleases (Eph. 4:7).... 'Tis his free and sovereign act that he doth so; he gives *higher degrees of glory* as a reward to the higher degrees of good works, not because it deserves it but because it pleases him.[18]

Proportioning the degrees of glory contains, furthermore, four aspects. First, there are degrees of grace and holiness

> not only the degree of the principle, but of the exercises and fruits, God will reward a principle of grace, as well as punish a principle of corruption, or a corrupt nature; and God will also reward all the exercises and fruits of grace, for all these are good works.[19]

---

17. *WJE* 13:436. Emphasis mine.
18. *WJE* 13:437. Emphasis mine.
19. *WJE* 13:527.

Second, "by which the degree [of] glory is proportioned is the degree of good that is done by the exercise and fruits of grace: the *degree of glory* to the name of God, and the degree of good done to men, especially to the household of faith." "How much," writes Edwards,

> is this way of doing good spoken of as a way of laying up trea-sure in heaven, and "laying up in store a good foundation against the time which is to come" (1 Tim. 6:17–19). And espe-cially giving to the poor saints, or members of Christ: Christ says that what is done to them he shall look upon as done to himself... [Matt. 25:40].[20]

Third, there are, for Edwards,

> Future degrees of glory [that] will be in proportion to [a] person's self-denial and suffering in the exercises and fruits of grace: for when grace is exercised and manifested in this manner, it is especially to the glory of God, for hereby the creature makes a sacrifice of himself and all things to the Creator...1 Peter 4:13, "But rejoice, inasmuch as ye are partakers of Christ's sufferings; that, when his glory shall be revealed, ye may be glad also with exceeding joy."[21]

Finally, what Edwards calls, "eminency in humility" consists in the degree of love. The exercise of love may be expressed in exalt-ing God; and God, "may especially be concerned to *reward* this by exalting and glorifying the subject of such exercises." So Edwards explains,

> in suffering so in humility, the saint does as it were lose [him-self]; he denies himself; he casts away himself; he renounces his own glory for God. Now God, in the reward, is concerned to make up this loss.[22]

Thus, the *degree of glory* is, on the one hand, a sovereign work of God, and on the other hand, an unmerited future reward to the saints. In fact, Edwards suggests that the saints will be higher in glory than the angels. In the same winter of 1739, he notes that

---

20. *WJE* 13:527. Emphasis mine.
21. *WJE* 13:528.
22. *WJE* 13:528.

the angels will be superior in greatness, in strength and wisdom, and so in that honor that belongs to 'em on that [account]; but they will not be superior in beauty and amiableness, and in being most beloved of God, and most nearly united to him, and having the fullest and sweetest enjoyment of him…. The saints will be superior in goodness and happiness, they will have the most excellent superiority. Goodness is more excellent than creature greatness; 'tis more divine. God communicates— [glorifies] himself more immediately in it.[23]

It is interesting to note that in the winter months of 1739 Edwards reflected on "glory," "beauty," "sweetness," and "heaven." Having finished three long sermon cycles, known as "The Parable of the Wise and Foolish Virgins," "Charity and Its Fruits," and "A History of the Work of Redemption," in the hope of reviving his backsliding congregation after the Connecticut Valley revival (ca. 1735–1737), the preacher of Northampton was discouraged. He writes to the British revivalist George Whitefield (1714–1770) in February 1740,

My request to you is that, in your intended journey through New England the next summer, you would be pleased to visit Northampton. I hope it is not wholly from curiosity that I desire to see and hear you in this place; but I apprehend, from what I have heard, that you are one that has the blessing of heaven attending you wherever you go; and I have a great desire, if it may be the will of God, that such a blessing as attends your person and labors may descend on this town, and may enter mine own house, and that I may receive it in my own soul. Indeed I am fearful whether you will not be disappointed in New England, and will have less success here than in other places: we who have dwelt in a land that has been distinguished with light, and have long enjoyed the gospel, and have been glutted with it, and have despised it, are I fear more hardened than most of those places where you have preached hitherto.[24]

Edwards and most of New England, however, were not disappointed. By the Spirit's grace, the coming of Whitefield in 1741 inaugurated the Great Awakening, and Edwards was swept up in the revival—becoming an itinerant preacher, counselor, and encourager

---

23. *WJE* 18:535.
24. *WJE* 16:80.

of New England's revival. Yet, the theme of glory had not left him, as he continued to reflect that the saints in heaven shall partake of Christ's own happiness and glory,[25] noting also that the glory of heaven was advanced at Christ's ascension.[26]

Did the hundreds of spiritually renewed and revived people of New England heighten Edwards's expectation of the hoped-for glorious millennium? Not necessarily, as even after his dismissal from the Northampton pastorate, he takes up the theme. In one of his last writings, *Dissertation Concerning the End for Which God Created the World*, he asserts, "God [is] glorifying himself, that glorifying himself which is the end of the creation."[27] That end goal of God's work is the glory of God and is, according to the then missionary at Stockbridge, "not only [a] manifestation of his excellency but [a] communication of his happiness."[28] God seeks occasions to exercise His goodness, and opportunities to communicate happiness, and this is one reason He gives being to creatures. And God, in seeking to exercise His goodness and communicate happiness, makes Himself His end. The end is Himself, in two respects, says Edwards:

> [God] himself flows forth; and he himself is pleased and gratified. For God's pleasure all things are and were created. God had made intelligent creatures capable of being concerned in these effects, as being the willing, active subjects or means, and so they are capable of actively promoting God's glory. And this is what they ought to make their ultimate end in all things.[29]

The theme of glory, then, remained a preoccupied concern throughout Edwards's life. The great work of redemption was understood as the ultimate display of the divine glory. In turn, Christ's bride shares in and is directed to that glory in creation, through redemption, and to consummation. In sum, Edwards's thought resonates with the first question and answer of the Westminster Catechism (1646): "What is the chief and highest end of man? Man's chief and highest end is

---

25. *WJE* 23:217–21.
26. *WJE* 23:229.
27. *WJE* 23:151.
28. *WJE* 23:222–24.
29. *WJE* 23:153.

glorifie God and fully enjoy him forever"[30]—words that echo Calvin's *Catechism of Geneva* (1545).[31]

Edwards's Sense of the Beauty of God

"The key to Edwards's thought is that everything is related because everything is related to God. Truth, a dimension of God's love and *beauty*, is part of that quintessentially bright light that pours forth from the throne of God."

Thus, George Marsden, in the most recent biography on Edwards,[32] notes that for Edwards creation functions as a school, training the regenerate in the "apprehension of God's glory mirrored in the beauty of the world."[33] Nature educates us about God's beauty, and it is sin that makes ugly what God created to reflect and to share His beauty. This reality of sin did not stop Edwards from maintaining an overarching concern "with God as an absolute *beauty* to be *enjoyed* [more] than with God as an absolute power to be feared,"[34] which runs contrary to the popular opinion of Edwards as a hellfire-and-brimstone preacher. In fact, his concern for nature and the natural phenomena was held early on in life, as noted in papers dated in the 1720s, titled, "Of the Rainbow," "Of Light Rays," "Wisdom in the Contrivance of the World," and last but not least, "Beauty of the World." The latter could be dated at "the end of Edwards's Yale tutorship, perhaps in the summer of 1726 or not long afterward."[35] The essay offers a window in Edwards's life-long thinking on beauty, stating in the opening paragraph,

---

30. *The Larger Catechism: first agreed upon by the Assembly of Divines at Westminster, and now approved by the Generall Assembly of the Kirk of Scotland, to be a part of uniformity in religion, between the kirks of Christ in the three kingdoms. Together with the Solemn league and covenant of the three kingdoms* (First printed at Edinburgh and now printed at London for the Company of Stationers, 1651), 73.

31. Jean Calvin, *Le Catechisme de Genêve* (Geneve: Jean Girard, 1549), 3: "Le ministre: Quelle est la principle fin de la vie humaine? L'Enfant: C'est de cognoistre Dieu. Le ministre: Pourquoy dis-tu cela? L'Enfant: Pource qu'il nous creé & mis au monde, pour ester glorifié en nous. Est c'est bien raison, que nous rapportons nostre vie à sa gloire: puis qu'il e nest le commencement."

32. George M. Marsden, *Jonathan Edwards: A Life* (New Haven: Yale University, 2003), 460. Emphasis mine.

33. Belden C. Lane, "Jonathan Edwards on Beauty, Desire, and the Sensory World," *Theological Studies* 65 (2004): 44.

34. Lane, "Jonathan Edwards on Beauty," 47. Emphasis mine.

35. *WJE* 6:297.

The beauty of the world consists wholly of sweet mutual consents, either within itself, or with the Supreme Being. As to the corporeal world, though there are many other sorts of consents, yet the sweetest and most charming beauty of it is its resemblance of spiritual beauties. The reason is that spiritual beauties are infinitely the greatest, and bodies being but the shadows of beings, they must be so much the more charming as they shadow forth spiritual beauties. This beauty is peculiar to natural things, it surpassing the art of man.[36]

Here one notes that Edwards understands beauty in relational terms as "[a] sweet mutual consent," either to itself or God. The latter, or spiritual beauties, are by far "the sweetest and most charming," "infinitely the greatest," and "surpassing the art of man," compared with the natural world. In fact, for Edwards the natural world is a shadow or type of the spiritual world and beauty. This should not lead to a hasty inference that Edwards disregards the natural world or creation. On the contrary, he notes in the essay,

'Tis very probable that that wonderful suitableness of green for the grass and plants, the blue of the sky, the white of the clouds, the colors of flowers, consists in a complicated proportion that these colors make one with another, either in the magnitude of the rays, the number of vibrations that are caused in the optic nerve, or some other way. So there is a great suitableness between the objects of different senses, as between sounds, colors, and smells—as between the colors of the woods and flowers, and the smell, and the singing of birds—which 'tis probable consist in a certain proportion of the vibrations that are made in the different organs. So there are innumerable other agreeablenesses of motions, figures, etc.: the gentle motions of trees, of lily, etc., as it is agreeable to other things that represent calmness, gentleness and benevolence, etc. The fields and woods seem to rejoice, and how joyful do the birds seem to be in it.[37]

This elaborate meditation on the beauty of the world is followed by a short sentence directing the reader to the spiritual realm,

How a resemblance, I say, of every grace and beautiful disposition of mind; of an inferior towards a superior cause, preserver,

---

36. *WJE* 6:305.
37. *WJE* 6:305.

benevolent benefactor, and a fountain of happiness. How great
a resemblance of a holy and virtuous soul in a calm serene day.[38]

Furthermore, Edwards says, beauty contains "harmony" and a
"proportionate mixture that is harmonious," appealing to the physi-
cist and mathematician, Isaac Newton (1643–1727). And it is likewise
the case in the spiritual realm: from the moment of regeneration
one's spiritual life is re-ordered, imparted with a new disposition to
be in harmony with its Creator. Just as the beauty of a person's body,
countenance, gesture, or voice charms us because it is the immediate
effect and emanation of an internal mental beauty, so the beauties of
nature are communications of God's excellencies, which find their
apex in the "excellencies of Christ."[39] Accordingly, Edwards writes in
a *Treatise Concerning Religious Affections* (1746) that a spiritual understanding is identified with the *new spiritual sense* or the sense which
apprehends the beauty and moral excellence of divine things.[40] That
is to say, true beauty is located in God and not in the eye of the
believer, although Edwards believed that only the purified and spiritual eye could apprehend it. The new sense is a taste of the beauty of
divine glory. This taste of beauty leads to another aspect: holiness.
Edwards identified the beauty of the divine nature with holiness,
as Scripture speaks of the "beauty of holiness" (Ps. 96:9). Therefore,
spiritual understanding consists primarily in a sense of the heart of
that spiritual beauty,[41] resulting in a life desiring holiness. But we
hear Edwards asking himself,

> Is my spiritual affection arising from a grasp of the beauty of
> holiness, based on the consideration that it is something profit-
> able for me *(bonum utile)*, or does it find its ground in the divine
> holiness as a "beautiful good in itself" *(bonum formosum)*?[42]

He underscores this distinction in part three of *Religious Affections*, "Showing What Are Distinguishing Signs of Truly Gracious
and Holy Affections," noting, "Nebuchadnezzar had a great and
very affecting sense of the infinite greatness and awful majesty of

---

38. *WJE* 6:306.
39. Cf. *WJE* 6:307, n. 1.
40. *WJE* 2:32.
41. *WJE* 2:272.
42. *WJE* 2:29–30.

God...and also had a great conviction in his conscience of his justice, and an affecting sense of his great goodness" (Dan. 4:1–3, 34–35, 37).[43] However, Edwards concludes that, without seeing or grasping God's beauty and the beauty of holiness, "the enmity of the heart will remain in its full strength, and no love will be enkindled." In contrast,

> The saints and angels do behold the glory of God consisting in the *beauty of his holiness*: and 'tis this sight only, that will melt and humble the hearts of men, and wean them from the world, and draw them to God, and effectually change them.... The first glimpse of the moral and spiritual glory of God shining into the heart, produces all these effects, as it were with omnipotent power, which nothing can withstand.[44]

In other words, a seeing of the beauty of God and His holiness with spiritual eyes is a transformative experience. It affects life and the disposition of life, as it works humility of heart, turning away from sin and turning to God—prompting a genuine evangelical repentance. God's beauty and glory cannot be withstood, and His grace tends to holy practice.[45]

This transformative and changing effect of the divine beauty in one's life was articulated by Edwards in September of 1752. He delivered a sermon before the Presbyterian Synod of New York, then assembled in Newark, New Jersey. The Congregational preacher and missionary at Stockbridge reminded his Presbyterian hearers and fellow-ministers:

> A sight of the greatness of God in his attributes, may overwhelm men, and be more than they can endure; but the enmity and opposition of the heart, may remain in its full strength, and the will remain inflexible; whereas, one glimpse of the moral and spiritual glory of God, and supreme amiableness of Jesus Christ, shining into the heart, overcomes and abolishes this opposition, and inclines the soul to Christ, as it were, by an omnipotent power: so that now, not only the understanding, but the will, and the whole soul receives and embraces the Savior.[46] This sense of divine beauty, is the first thing in the actual change made in the

---

43. *WJE* 2:264.
44. *WJE* 2:264–65.
45. Cf. *WJE* 8:294.
46. *WJE* 25:625.

soul, in true conversion, and is the foundation of everything else belonging to that change; as is evident by those words of the Apostle, 2 Corinthians 3:18, "But we all with open face, beholding as in a glass, the glory of the Lord, are changed into the same image, from glory to glory, even as by the Spirit of the Lord."[47]

Why, then, is glory and beauty of such importance to Edwards? It was the sum of the gospel culminating in Christ, as he wrote to Lady Pepperrell near Boston, to console her on the loss of her son:

'Tis the glory and beauty of his love to us filthy sinners, that 'tis an infinitely pure love and it tends to the peculiar sweetness and endearment of his infinite holiness; that it has its greatest manifestation in such an act of love to us…. And we have this friend, this mighty Redeemer…who is not one that can't be touched with the feeling of our afflictions, he having suffered far greater sorrows than we ever have done…. In him we may triumph with everlasting joy; even when storms and tempests arise we may have resort to him who is an hiding place from the wind and a covert from the tempest. When we are thirsty, we may come to him who is as rivers of waters in a dry place. When we are weary, we may go to him who is as the shadow of a great rock in a weary land…. He will be [our] light in darkness and [our] morning star that is a bright harbinger of day. And in a little [while], he will arise on our souls as the sun in full glory. And our sun shall no more go down, and there shall be no interposing cloud, no veil on his face or on our hearts, but the Lord shall be our everlasting light and our Redeemer, our glory.[48]

The Surprise of Beauty and Glory

Having explored preliminarily *what* God's "glory" and "beauty" is for Edwards, I come to the last point: *Why* is he surprised by it? For this I have selected three periods in his life: before, during, and after the revivals (the Connecticut Valley revival of the mid-1730s and the Great Awakening of the early 1740s) — in other words, the beginning, middle, and end of Edwards's life.

Edwards was the son of the Rev. Timothy Edwards (1669–1758) and Esther Stoddard (1673–1770) — daughter of the famous pastor Solomon Stoddard (1643–1729) of Northampton. Dubbed the "pope

---

47. *WJE* 25:626.
48. *WJE* 16:418–19.

of New England," Edwards in his early years was very much concerned that he did not fit the usual Puritan paradigm of conversion, a "preparationism" where unregenerate people were urged to take steps in preparation for conversion. Although such preparatory work was accredited to the work of Holy Spirit when it was salvific, Edwards distanced himself from one of the premier promoters of preparationism, his grandfather Solomon Stoddard. That is not to say he was unaffected by the ministry of his grandfather, as he attests in his *Personal Narrative* as having "remarkable seasons of awakening, before I met with that change, by which I was brought to those new dispositions, and that new sense of things."[49]

In fact, he was concerned about the things of religion and his soul's salvation, "and was abundant in duties," writing, "I used to pray five times a day in secret, and to spend much time in religious talk with other boys; and used to meet with them to pray together."[50] But over time, his convictions and affections wore off; he entirely lost all "those affections and delights," and left off secret prayer.[51]

Hence, to his surprise, while reading 1 Timothy 1:17, "Now unto the King eternal, immortal, invisible, the only wise God, be honor and glory forever and ever, Amen," he recalls, "there came into my soul, and was as it were diffused through it, a sense of the glory of the divine being; a new sense, quite different from anything I ever experienced before. Never any words of Scripture seemed to me as these words did."[52]

He continues,

> I began to have a new kind of apprehensions and ideas of Christ, and the work of redemption, and the glorious way of salvation by him. I had an inward, sweet sense of these things, that at times came into my heart; and my soul was led away in pleasant views and contemplations of them. And my mind was greatly engaged, to spend my time in reading and meditating on Christ; and the beauty and excellency of his person, and the lovely way of salvation, by free grace in him.[53]

---

49. *WJE* 16:790.
50. *WJE* 16:790.
51. Cf. *WJE* 16:791 paraphrased.
52. *WJE* 16:792.
53. *WJE* 16:793.

In other words, despite his initial religious feelings and inclinations and losing all interest in the things of religion, Edwards experienced being "wrapt and swallowed up in God" unexpectedly and surprisingly, while reading Scripture. Recalling that day, he notes having "a [surprising] sweet sense of the glorious majesty and grace of God, that I know not how to express. I seemed to see them both in a sweet conjunction: majesty and meekness joined together: it was a sweet and gentle, and holy majesty; and also a majestic meekness; an awful sweetness; a high, and great, and holy gentleness."

This surprising experience of the glory and beauty of God stands in stark contrast to what he wrote earlier in his "Diary," saying, "I cannot speak so fully to my experience of that preparatory work, of which divines speak." In his last and lasting statement on spiritual discernment, Edwards counsels in *Religious Affections,*

> Nothing can certainly be determined that comforts and joys seem to follow awakenings and convictions of conscience, in a *certain order*...a method, as has been much insisted on by many divines; *first*, such awakenings, fears and awful apprehensions followed with such legal humblings, in a sense of total sinfulness and helplessness, and *then*, such and such light and comfort....[54]

Edwards writes of his conversion, appealing almost poetically to the spring, sun, and senses:

> The soul of a true Christian, as I then wrote my meditations, appeared like such a little white flower, as we see in the spring of the year; low and humble on the ground, opening its bosom, to receive the pleasant beams of the sun's glory; rejoicing as it were, in a calm rapture; diffusing around a sweet fragrancy; standing peacefully and lovingly, in the midst of other flowers round about; all in like manner opening their bosoms, to drink in the light of the sun.[55]

In addition to *Religious Affections*, Edwards wrote three other works aimed at interpreting and discerning the work of the Spirit in New England: *A Faithful Narrative of the Surprising Work of God* (1737), *The Distinguishing Marks of a Work of the Spirit of God* (1741), and

---

54. *WJE* 2:151.
55. *WJE* 16:796.

Some Thoughts Concerning the Present Revival of Religion in New England (1742). These works on the revivals, which are for Edwards "to record and publish this surprising work of God,"[56] have in common his understanding that the grace of God, the work of redemption, and the work of the Spirit is surprising, considering the lost state of humanity. Already in a sermon titled, "Christians a Chosen Generation," he ponders that

> The grace of God in the work of redemption, when it is seen in its true light discovered by divine and spiritual light to the soul, will evermore appear wonderful. It will appear a wonderful thing that God should so pity, and that Christ should so love, such sinful worms of the dust, to come into the world and take on him the human nature, and lay down his life. Thinking much of this, and conversing much of it, and continuing to praise God for it, will never make it grow old; but it will seem wonderful and surprising. There is wonderfulness and glory enough in it to keep the souls of saints and angels forever in admiration and rapture.[57]

In a letter to Benjamin Colman, a minister in Boston, Edwards voices his amazement about what happened during the time from the winter of 1734 to the spring of 1735:

> There began to be a *remarkable* religious concern among some farm houses...then a concern about the great things of religion began.... Then the people in New Hadley seemed to be *seized* with a deep concern about their salvation.... This town [Northampton] never was so *full of love*, nor so *full of joy*.... Many express a sense of the glory of the divine perfections, and of the excellency and fullness of Jesus Christ, and of their own littleness and unworthiness, in a manner truly wonderful and almost unparalleled.[58]

Although the last observation parallels his own conversion, Edwards continues to emphasize this *"surprising* and wonderful" work of God

---

56. *WJE* 4:140.

57. *WJE* 17:324. Sermon May 1731, "Christians a Chosen Generation," "But ye are a chosen generation, a royal priesthood, an holy nation, a peculiar people; that ye should show forth the praises of him who hath called you out of darkness into marvelous light" (1 Peter 2:9).

58. *WJE* 16:50–54.

in various sermons during this time, such as "Underserved Mercies," and "Excellencies of Christ."[59]

This notion of "surprise," amazement, astonishment, and wonder about the natural ("Beauty of the World") and the supernatural (the saving work of the Spirit) was present life-long in Edwards. Surprised at the time of his own conversion, and surprised by God's work in the life of hundreds of people in the times of the revival, he remained amazed at the end of his life, remarking on a revival at the College of New Jersey (Princeton University). He writes to his Scottish correspondent, the Rev. John Erskine of Edinburgh, "A great and glorious work is going on in college. God is evidently here in a surprising manner."[60]

Conclusion: The Effect of the Beauty and Glory of God

In conclusion, Edwards spoke and wrote much throughout his life on being surprised by the beauty and glory of God. Yet, he once commented, "I know not how to express [it]." Whether it was the rays of the light of nature (see essay "Of Light Rays")[61] or the divine and supernatural light, it was a beauty and glory of God that was to be seen, tasted, and experienced. The spiritual beauties, however, are infinitely the greater: They "delight us and we can't tell why," says Edwards, but "some image of the beauty of Christ [is] derived upon [our] soul; it appears in [our] words and actions, and may be seen in [our] life and walk."[62] Being affected by the beauty and glory of God in Christ, is *seen* in one's life—in word and deed. It was something he had seen in Sarah Pierpont, while he was a student and tutor at Yale College,

> They say there is a young lady in [New Haven].... She is of a wonderful sweetness, calmness and universal benevolence of mind; especially after those times in which this great [glorious] God has manifested himself to her mind. She will sometimes go about, singing sweetly, from place to [place]; and seems to be always full of joy and pleasure.[63]

---

59. See for example, the sermons "Undeserved Mercy" (*WJE* 19:640), and "The Excellencies of Christ" (*WJE* 19:589).

60. *WJE* 16:704.

61. *WJE* 6:302–304.

62. *WJE* 10:572.

63. *WJE* 16:789.

She became his wife, who wrote to her daughter Esther upon the death of Jonathan Edwards at Princeton in March 1758, "O what a legacy my husband, and your father, has left us! We are all given to God; and there I am, and love to be."[64] What a legacy—and yet, let's each of us continue to be surprised by the *same* beauty and glory of God, and may these be *seen* in our lives.

---

64. *WJE* 32:C146. Sarah Pierpont Edwards to Esther Edwards Burr, 4/3/58. ANTS, f. 1756-59C, #9, C, #4.

CHAPTER 10

Thomas Boston on the Last Things

William VanDoodewaard

Thomas Boston is perhaps best remembered as the Scottish Presbyterian theologian who led efforts to recover the gospel of the Lord Jesus Christ in the days of the Marrow controversy, through his appreciation for and use of *The Marrow of Modern Divinity*. He stands as a familiar champion of the complete sufficiency of Christ as Savior of sinners, the free offer of the gospel, the scriptural relationship of law and gospel, and life in union with Christ. Other areas of his life and ministry are less known, including his personal preparation for death, and his pastoral care for his congregation in relation to the last things—death and what follows.

Preparing for Exit

In November 1729, at 53 years of age, Boston's health was in substantial decline. Seriously ill, he sensed his life might not last much longer. Despite some seasons of relief and improvement, he would die May 20, 1732, at the age of 56. Having just finished a substantial writing project in the midst of his busy pastoral ministry, he now wrote in his journal "considering that I had now no more of that kind of work ahead of me, I devoted myself to setting matters in order for my departure out of this world, and for pursuing the essay on the Hebrew text after that, if my life would continue longer."[1]

As interesting as his work on the Hebrew text might be, this essay follows Boston's lead, with the goal of preparing us for our own departure from this world. His following journal entries provide us

---

1. Thomas Boston, *Memoirs of the Life, Times, and Writings of Thomas Boston of Ettrick* (Glasgow: John M'Neilage, 1899), 412. Quotations have been edited and updated for the reader.

with a good beginning point. Boston spent time in prayer and fast-
ing on December 2, 1729, "in order to prepare for death."[2] After his
ordinary morning devotions that day he read some Scripture passages, reflected on two confessions of sin he had written thirty years
earlier, and then used the Larger Catechism on the Ten Command-
ments as a help in praying through confessing his sin to the Lord: "I
prayed and made confession of my sins as fully and particularly as
I could; and there I got a view of my whole life as one heap of vanity, sin, and foolishness.... It cut to the heart to think of it."[3] He then
re-read two private pieces he had written in 1699 and 1700, personal
covenants of faith, taking hold of the covenant of grace in Christ.
Looking back again he was reminded that he had had "more dark
views...of the covenant of grace" in the early part of his ministry,
and in prayer he took hold again "of God's covenant of grace for life
and salvation to me."

A few days later Boston spent further time in personal preparation for his death. He read through Scripture passages on God's
gospel promises in Christ, reflected on the death of his physical body,
and meditated upon the resurrection. "Rising up from prayer, filled
with joy in believing, I sang with an exalting heart...and set myself
to gather some evidences for heaven."[4]

What did Boston mean by spending time "gathering evidences
for heaven"? He did not mean finding proofs for the existence for
heaven; he meant looking to the Word and to the Spirit's work in
his life both to examine where he was spiritually, and also to gain
assurance of the sure hope of heaven in and through Christ and His
work within him. As he did on this Thursday afternoon in the chill
of the Scottish winter, likely bundled up and seated near a fireplace
or stove, he recorded seven points of personal reflection:

1. I see that I believe the Gospel, with application to myself; and
   find that my expectations from it do ultimately resolve themselves on the faithfulness of God in the word of the promise
   of the Gospel. The which is a good evidence according to Isaiah 53:1; John 3:33–36; Hebrews 10:23; 2 Timothy 1:12.

---

2. Boston, *Memoirs*, 414.
3. Boston, *Memoirs*, 414.
4. Boston, *Memoirs*, 416.

2. I find that my soul rests in, and is grateful for the covenant of grace, as God's plan of salvation in Christ; and that I have come into it with heart and will; taking my offered place in it in Christ the Second Adam, putting down my little name within the compass of His great and glorious name. By this I know I, as a member of the mystical body of the Second Adam, am as really entitled to the promise of the covenant of grace, eternal life, made to Him for all His, as I was rendered liable to the penalty of the broken covenant of works, eternal death, in the First Adam (2 Samuel 23:5; Isaiah 56:4–5; 1 Corinthians 1:24; Matthew 6:6; Romans 5:19).

3. I find my heart is so much at odds with sin, that if there were no other hell, but just being left in sin forever, "he that is filthy, let him be filthy still," my heart would, on that sentence against me, break in a thousand pieces. Is not this the work of the sanctifying Spirit of Christ in me? (Romans 7:23–25 and 8:6; Galatians 5:17).

4. I have a hope of heaven, through Jesus Christ; and the Lord knows it moves me to desire, long, and seek to be made fit for it, in purification from sin (1 John 3:3).

5. I love the purity of the divine image expressed in the holy law, and every line of it, so far as I discern it; even where it strikes against the sin that most easily besets me (Hebrews 8:10; Psalm 119:6; Romans 7:22).

6. I have some confidence, that I will receive complete life and salvation; but that confidence is not in myself; for God knows I know, that of all the periods of my life, any one would undoubtedly ruin me, and that most justly. So I have no confidence of acceptance with God, but in Christ crucified, who loved me, and gave Himself for me.

7. Finally [regarding the sin I have often struggled with] and which has often threatened to baffle all my evidences for heaven, as the one thing lacking; I can say, I sincerely desire to get above it, be forever done with it, and take Christ in its place. I have sometimes got above it, from spiritual principles, motives, and ends. It has often influenced and directed me…. I am heartily ashamed of that before the Lord…at the

same time it has contributed to empty me, shake me out of myself, and drive me to Christ. I love God in Christ above it.[5]

Following these self-reflections, mixed with prayer, Boston prayed some more, now about the separation of his soul from his body and "my removal from this world" as well as "the resurrection of my body at the last day." "I did particularly beg," Boston records, "that, having lived so little to His glory, He would enable me to die to His glory."[6] He prayed that the Lord would give him patience, should his illness to death last long, and that if it was the Lord's will, He would give him the ability to speak till his death, but if not, "that my countenance might speak to His glory."[7]

Boston's careful preparation for his own death reflected patterns evident in a lifetime of ministry to his congregations, first at Simprin, and then Ettrick. In a sermon on Ephesians 4:13 published in 1708 he noted that "the office and work of the ministry is to continue till all the elect of God are fully perfected, and the church arrives at its full growth."[8] It was evident he meant that this work was to be pursued by ministers like himself, both in encouraging their hearers to a growing life in Christ, and in instilling the same biblical vision within them. The goal of the Christian life was clearly the pursuit of holiness in union with Christ, longing for, and anticipating the day of full perfection in His glorious presence. Fittingly, in his *Fourfold State of Man*, based on a sermon series in Ettrick between 1708–9, Boston emphasized and expounded the believer's mystical union with Christ, before turning to consider death and the eternal state of man.

Shepherding for Eternity
Death

Taking Job 30:23, with its acknowledgment of the impending, God-appointed reality of death, Boston stated "all men must, by death, be removed out of this world, they must die."[9] "The appointment [with

---

5. Boston, *Memoirs*, 416–18.

6. Boston, *Memoirs*, 418.

7. Boston, *Memoirs*, 418.

8. Thomas Boston, "Ministers to Continue till the Church be Perfect" in *The Complete Works of Thomas Boston*, vol. 4 (Stoke-on-Trent: Tentmaker Publications, 2002), 316.

9. Thomas Boston, *The Fourfold State of Man* (Edinburgh: Banner of Truth, 2002), 323.

death] cannot be shifted; it is a law which mortals cannot transgress."[10] In another sermon preached around the same time in Ettrick, Boston brought this reality home, reminding his hearers, "We do not only read of the certainty of our death in our Bibles, but in our own bodies, where every pain and weakness are reminders of approaching death."[11] At the same time he cautioned them that being "healthy, strong, lively, and vigorous, may seem to be far from death," yet it is not unusual at all to see sudden deaths.[12] He also reminded them of the fact that they did not know how soon they would die.

Boston encouraged his hearers to make use of the approaching reality of their own deaths as a motive to steadfastness and growth in Christ, as well as to self-examination: "your eternal state will be according to the state in which you die.... If one dies out of Christ, in an unregenerate state, there is no hope for him forever.... Our life in this world is but a short preface to a long eternity."[13] Make sure, he urged, that you are united to Jesus Christ by faith; until you are you cannot die in peace.[14] Turning from the general topic of death, Boston next considers "the difference between the righteous and the wicked in their death."[15] Where the righteous in Christ have hope in their death, the wicked in dying "are driven away in their wickedness, and in a hopeless state."[16] As Boston unpacks these truths he is quick to note to his hearers that "if you are not righteous, you are wicked."[17] If you are still not united to Christ by faith, no matter how morally upstanding your life appears to others, you are among the wicked who will be banished to hell, if death comes to you while you are still apart from Him. He urges his hearers "to flee to Jesus Christ as the all-sufficient Savior, [the] almighty Redeemer."[18] On the contrary, Boston encouraged his hearers that for all who trust in Christ, who

---

10. Boston, *Fourfold State*, 323.

11. Thomas Boston, "Readiness for our Removal into the Other World Opened Up, Urged, and Enforced" in *The Complete Works of Thomas Boston*, vol. 5 (Stoke-on-Trent: Tentmaker Publications, 2002), 559–60.

12. Boston, "Readiness for our Removal," 561.

13. Boston, *Fourfold State*, 338.

14. Boston, *Fourfold State*, 339.

15. Boston, *Fourfold State*, 340.

16. Boston, *Fourfold State*, 340–41.

17. Boston, *Fourfold State*, 342.

18. Boston, *Fourfold State*, 352.

are united to him by faith, their deaths are "happy and hopeful."[19] They have a trustworthy good Friend in the world they are entering. Boston said, "I think, when the Lord calls a godly man out of the world, He sends him such good news, and such a kind invitation to the other world, that, having faith to believe it, his spirit must revive, when he sees the Lord has sent death to bring him there."[20]

There is a sober and weighty aspect to what is coming: "after death the judgment."[21] As the Christian thinks of this he will realize, "more deeply than others," the profound seriousness of what is happening; and will also realize more deeply the reality of his own sin.[22] Satan will do his utmost to rob them of peace as they face the last enemy.[23] But Boston reminds us, their case is entirely positive for Christ is their Lord, their Husband, and their Judge, and as Judge, is also their Advocate. They do not need to have any fear of condemnation, for not only is Christ their Judge and Advocate, He is also their Redeemer. They are "redeemed with the precious blood of Christ" (1 Peter 1:18–19).[24]

While noting the reality that they do have to go through the valley of the shadow of death, Boston encourages, "Death can do them no harm. It cannot even hurt their bodies, for though it separates the soul from the body, it cannot separate the body from the Lord Jesus Christ."[25] Jesus Christ has abolished death—"the soul and life of it is gone"; it is simply a shadow which may cause fear, but cannot hurt the Christian. "The nature of death is quite changed for the saints; it is not to them what it was to Jesus Christ their head.[26] The sting has been removed, so that it becomes the way into a joyful entrance into the other world.[27] Boston said, "Their arrival in the regions of bliss will be celebrated with rapturous hymns of praise to their glorious Redeemer. A dying day is a good day for a godly man. Yes, it is his best day; it is better for him than the day of his birth, or the most joyful day he ever had on earth."[28] Death is one of the "all things"

---

19. Boston, *Fourfold State*, 353.
20. Boston, *Fourfold State*, 353.
21. Boston, *Fourfold State*, 353.
22. Boston, *Fourfold State*, 359.
23. Boston, *Fourfold State*, 359.
24. Boston, *Fourfold State*, 353.
25. Boston, *Fourfold State*, 354–55.
26. Boston, *Fourfold State*, 355.
27. Boston, *Fourfold State*, 356.
28. Boston, *Fourfold State*, 356.

that work together for good to those that love God—something Boston explores in greater detail in sermons titled "The Benefits Which Believers Receive at Death."[29]

While our souls are separated from our bodies at death, even our dead bodies as they rest and decay in the grave are not separated from Christ; they remain precious to Him, and He will raise and reunite us with them.[30] While we leave our bodies behind, we will experience immediate perfection of holiness, with perfect and permanent freedom from all sin and its effects. Our understanding will be perfectly illuminated: "Then I shall know even as I am known."[31] Our wills will be perfectly upright. We will enter a paradise of sweet fellowship. Through our immediate entrance into a glorious place, into heaven, we will join the community of the saints made perfect, the angels, the "glorious Mediator [and] the blessed Trinity."[32]

In the last part of his section on death in the *Fourfold State*, Boston, with a pastoral heart, walks his readers through a number of case examples of struggles faced in death: worry about leaving family behind; being separated from our closest earthly friends; struggles with assurance of salvation; realization of spiritual decline rather than growth; fear of the unknown; fear of the physical pains of dying; fear of sudden death; fear of mental incapacity; fear that I am always fearful, and the doubt that I could ever make it through this.[33]

Boston concludes with practical advice on how Christians can prepare for death: 1) keep a clean conscience, walking close with God; 2) stay spiritually watchful; 3) seek to grow in living as a pilgrim in this world, guarding against being overly attached to its stuff; 4) examine yourself spiritually, asking God, through Christ, by His Spirit and Word, to enable you to do so. 5) Do the work the Lord has called you to with speed and diligence.[34]

---

29. Thomas Boston, "Of the Benefits Which Believers Receive at Death" in *The Complete Works of Thomas Boston*, vol. 2 (Stoke-on-Trent: Tentmaker Publications, 2002), 37–41.

30. Boston, "Of the Benefits Which Believers Receive at Death," 40.

31. Boston, "Of the Benefits Which Believers Receive at Death," 38.

32. Boston, "Of the Benefits Which Believers Receive at Death," 39.

33. Boston, *Fourfold State*, 361–64.

34. Boston, *Fourfold State*, 367–72.

The Resurrection and the Judgment

After his counsel on death in his book *The Fourfold State*, Thomas Boston considers both the resurrection and the final judgment. With pastoral heart he begins by impressing on us the certainty of the resurrection. It is a sure thing. "Cannot the great Creator, who made all things of nothing, raise man's body, after it has become dust?" If the objection is raised, "How can our bodies be raised again, after they have decayed to dust…?" Scripture and reason provide the answer, "For men it is impossible, but not for God…. God is omniscient and omnipotent, infinite in knowledge and power."[35] "This great work [of resurrection] appears most reasonable."[36] God in His omniscience, Boston says, knows where every little particle of our dust is, what it is, and in His omnipotence is able to bring the human body back together after its dissolution, just as He was able to form us from the dust of the earth and the rib in our creation in Adam and Eve.[37] Not only is He able to raise us from the dead, gloriously renewed and perfected, but God will do it: "He certainly will do it, because He has said it."[38]

Boston notes that it will not only be believers who are raised; all will be raised. However, "there is a great difference between the godly and the wicked, in their life, and in their death; so will there be also in their resurrection."[39] While believers are raised in union with Christ, and will be "with inexpressible joy," "the wicked shall be raised by the power of Christ, as a Just Judge, who is to render vengeance to His enemies."[40] "They will come forth from their graves with unspeakable horror and consternation…crying out to the mountains and rocks to fall on them, and hide them from the face of the Lamb."[41]

The resurrection is first of all a resurrection to judgment before Christ: both for believers and for the wicked. It will mark a clear and eternal separation. "God will bring every work into judgement, with every secret thing, whether good or evil."[42] The saints in Christ will be brought into their eternal reward, while the sentence of damnation

---

35. Boston, *Fourfold State*, 375–76.
36. Boston, *Fourfold State*, 377.
37. Boston, *Fourfold State*, 377.
38. Boston, *Fourfold State*, 378.
39. Boston, *Fourfold State*, 382.
40. Boston, *Fourfold State*, 383–84.
41. Boston, *Fourfold State*, 385.
42. Boston, *Fourfold State*, 410.

will fall upon the wicked. Now as Boston preached and spoke on the last things, particularly as he addressed both the intermediate state (the state between death and the final resurrection and judgment), as well as the eternal future afterwards, he focused on two abiding destinies: heaven, for the believers, and hell for the unrepentant wicked.

Heaven and Hell

Boston draws tremendous encouragement for us from the Word as he helps us see the beautiful realities of the kingdom of heaven.[43] In June of 1707, Thomas Boston preached a sermon titled "Believers Seek a Continuing City" to his congregation at Ettrick. Reminding the congregation that we do not have a "continuing city" here, he urged them to anticipate and live towards "the one that is to come."[44] This city to come, he proclaimed, is built by God, and will endure forever. Jesus Christ is the eternal prophet, priest, and king of the city, and those who enter through faith and new life in Him receive immortality: "garments of glory" that will never be removed. Their privileges there will never end. There will be no sin or sinning there, and none of the miserable effects of sin. Death cannot enter.[45]

Heaven, Boston continues, will be a place of activity. It is a place of worship and service. Our work there will be "eternal recreation and perfect pleasure."[46] Heaven "is a kingdom that cannot be moved."[47] "The rest, quiet, and safety of that city are continuing."[48] It is a place of happiness, joy, and perfect prosperity. Above all, as Boston describes in his chapter on the kingdom of heaven in his *Fourfold State*, it is a place of perfect communion not only with saints and angels, but with God, in Christ. "Christ will grant them to sit with him" on His throne.[49] Heaven is the city that God has prepared for His people, the home He welcomes them to. "They shall have society with the Lord himself in heaven, glorious communion with God and Christ, which

---

43. While Boston speaks of the inauguration of the new creation as he describes Scripture's teaching on the kingdom of heaven, and of the resurrection of believers, his descriptive focus tends to be primarily on heaven in the intermediate state.

44. Thomas Boston, "Believers Seeking a Continuing City" in *The Complete Works of Thomas Boston* (Stoke-on-Trent: Tentmaker Publications, 2002), 247–61.

45. Boston, "Believers Seeking a Continuing City," 250.

46. Boston, "Believers Seeking a Continuing City," 251.

47. Boston, "Believers Seeking a Continuing City," 252.

48. Boston, "Believers Seeking a Continuing City," 252.

49. Boston, *Fourfold State*, 435.

is the perfection of happiness…so shall we ever be with the Lord."[50]
Boston explains this glorious communion the saints will enjoy:

> God is everywhere present in respect of his essence: the saints
> militant have his special gracious presence; but in heaven they
> have his glorious presence. There they are brought near to the
> throne of the great King, and stand before Him, where he shows
> his inconceivable glory. There they have the tabernacle of God,
> on which the cloud of glory rests, the all-glorious human nature
> of Christ, in which the fulness of the Godhead dwells; not veiled
> as in the days of his humiliation, but shining…that all his saints
> may behold his glory…who can conceive of the happiness of the
> saints in the presence…of the great King. The saints in heaven
> shall have the full enjoyment…all their wants…the desires of
> their souls, enjoying God and the Lamb in heaven.[51]

Boston urged his congregations, and his readers, that this is
worth living for, and worth dying for. Heaven can only be gained in
and through Christ, who freely welcomes and calls us to Himself. He
impressed the weightiness of our need to be in Christ through his
concluding chapter of the *Fourfold State* on the reality of hell, with all
the terror and awfulness of its unending reality of existence under
the holy wrath of God.[52]

Last Words
Still struggling along through illness in 1730, Thomas Boston wrote
the following words on October 28, to his children, John, Jane, Ali-
son, and Thomas Jr.:

> You [are] children of the covenant, devoted unto the God and
> Father of our Lord Jesus Christ…therefore I charge you to ratify
> the same with your own consent, and personal acceptance of
> the covenant, and to cleave to this God as your God, all the days
> of your lives, as being His only, wholly, and forever…the Lord
> bless each one of you, and save you, and cause His gracious face

---

50. Boston, *Fourfold State*, 449.

51. Boston, *Fourfold State*, 450–51.

52. Boston's treatment of hell appears to describe it as a place where the wicked
keep on sinning; a place of entire separation from God. Ted Donnelly provides a
more fully scriptural account in his *Biblical Teaching on the Doctrines of Heaven and
Hell* (Edinburgh: Banner of Truth, 2001), 16–47. He notes that hell is ruled by God
and exists for His glory; it is a place of His immediate presence "in his anger."

to shine on you, and give you peace; so as we may have a comfortable meeting in the other world! Farewell.[53]

The same year his final words in his journal stated:

> Thus I have given some account of the days of my vanity...upon the whole, I bless my God in Jesus Christ, that ever He made me a Christian, and took an early dealing with my soul; that ever He made me a minister of the Gospel, and gave me some insight into the doctrine of grace; and that ever He gave me the blessed Bible...[54]

Despite ongoing, slow deterioration, Boston continued to minister to his church; even preaching from the window in the manse when unable to get up to walk to the church. We don't know whether he preached on these specific topics in his final months and weeks, but undoubtedly these great truths and realities were often on his heart and mind as his body continued to deteriorate.

Less than two years after concluding his journal, at home in Ettrick, Thomas Boston had persevered to the finish, trusting in Christ his Savior. On "May 20, 1732...he entered into the joy of his Lord."[55]

---

53. Boston, Memoirs, 1-3.
54. Boston, Memoirs, 466.
55. Boston, Memoirs, 467.

EXPERIENTIAL STUDIES

CHAPTER 11

The Marriage of Christ and His Church

Joel R. Beeke

Have you ever noticed that the Bible does not speak about dying and going to heaven? It speaks about dying and going to be with Christ. Christ is the sum and substance of heaven's glory. Samuel Rutherford said, "Suppose that our Lord would manifest His art, and make ten thousand heavens of good and glorious things, and of new joys, devised out of the deep of infinite wisdom, He could not make the like of Christ."[1]

There are several reasons why heaven is so focused on our glorious Savior. One reason is that no one can get there without Christ's saving work. Anyone who enters heaven must confess with Anne Cousin:

> I stand upon His merit; I know no other stand,
> Not e'en where glory dwelleth in Immanuel's land.[2]

Christ is the centerpiece of heaven because in heaven, faith in Christ will become sight of Christ. Peter describes our present situation: We love a Christ whom we have not seen, "in whom, though now ye see him not, yet believing, ye rejoice with joy unspeakable and full of glory" (1 Peter 1:8). Faith in the unseen Christ will be rewarded by the joy of looking upon Him, and seeing Him as He is, forever. "Thine eyes shall see the king in his beauty" (Isa. 33:17).

Heaven is Christ-centered because in heaven every believer will be fully conformed to the image of Christ. We who believe "shall be like

---

1. *Letters of Samuel Rutherford*, ed. Andrew Bonar (1891; repr., Edinburgh: Banner of Truth, 1984), 413.

2. One of the nineteen original stanzas of "Immanuel's Land," Anne Cousin's hymn, first published in 1857, and composed of lines gathered from the *Letters and Dying Sayings* of Samuel Rutherford (d. 1661), published in 1664.

him" (1 John 3:2), and He shall be "the firstborn among many brethren" (Rom. 8:29). What bliss it will be to be without sin, and to reflect Christ so completely that it will be impossible to be un-Christlike!

Heaven is focused on Christ because His glory will always shine there, and His praises will never grow old. "And the city had no need of the sun, neither of the moon, to shine in it: for the glory of God did lighten it, and the Lamb is the light thereof" (Rev. 21:23).

But another, all-too-often-forgotten reason that heaven focuses on Christ is that in heaven the living church will be married to Christ and will express the love of a bride toward her husband. Dear believer, your engagement to Jesus Christ in this life will be turned into perfect marital union with Him in heaven. This theme often surfaces in Bible passages.[3] But nowhere is the theme of our marriage to Christ so beautifully unfolded as in Scripture's last chapters.

Revelation 19:7–9 says, "Let us be glad and rejoice, and give honour to him: for the marriage of the Lamb is come, and his wife hath made herself ready. And to her was granted that she should be arrayed in fine linen, clean and white: for the fine linen is the righteousness of saints. And he saith unto me, Write, Blessed are they which are called unto the marriage supper of the Lamb."

As *The Reformation Heritage KJV Study Bible* says, "Redemption is a love story (Isa. 54:4–8; Hos. 3:1–5), the covenant is a vow of betrothal (Hos. 2:19–20), salvation is a wedding dress (Isa. 61:10), and the kingdom is a wedding feast (Matt. 22:1–14)."[4] Let us consider what Revelation 19:7–9 says about the wedding, the Bridegroom, the bride, and the guests.

The Wedding

Presently, the church is betrothed and waiting for her wedding day. There is a difference between what we mean by engagement and what the Bible means by betrothal; betrothal (or espousal) in Bible times was like a very strong form of engagement which could not be broken. From the day they were betrothed to each other, the couple would be regarded as husband and wife, but they would not live

---

3. Ps. 45:10–15; Isa. 54:5; 62:4–5; Matt. 9:15; 25:1–13; John 3:28, 29; 2 Cor. 11:2; Eph. 5:22–33.

4. *The Reformation Heritage KJV Study Bible* (Grand Rapids: Reformation Heritage Books, 2014), 1892.

together. For example, Mary and Joseph were only "espoused" or betrothed, and he was shocked to discover that she was pregnant, but the angel called her his "wife" (Matt. 1:18, 20).[5] With the betrothal, the bridegroom would pay the bride's father a dowry, or "bride-price."[6] According to Jewish tradition, "the marriage agreement, drawn up at betrothal, was committed into the hands of the best man."[7] Then, when the wedding day came, both bride and groom would dress in fine clothing (Isa. 61:10). He would come to her home to get her and her friends, and take them to her new home, where they would all feast and celebrate for as long as a week (Judg. 14:12; Matt. 25:1–13).[8]

All Christians are betrothed to Christ. Paul was thus jealously protective of believers who were being troubled by false apostles who preached another gospel. He said in 2 Corinthians 11:2–4, "I am jealous over you with godly jealousy: for I have espoused you to one husband, that I may present you as a chaste virgin to Christ. But I fear, lest by any means, as the serpent beguiled Eve through his subtlety, so your minds should be corrupted from the simplicity that is in Christ. For if he that cometh preacheth another Jesus, whom we have not preached, or if ye receive another spirit, which ye have not received, or another gospel, which ye have not accepted, ye might well bear with him." Paul casts himself in the role of the marriage broker or matchmaker. In his love for Christ, he desires to present Him with a chaste virgin bride; in his concern for the Corinthians, he resents anyone who wants to lead them astray into spiritual adultery.

---

5. See also Deut. 20:7; 22:23–24; 28:30.

6. On the bride-price (KJV "dowry"), see Gen. 34:12; Ex. 22:16–17; 1 Sam. 18:25; cf. Deut. 22:28–29.

7. D. J. William, "Bride, Bridegroom," in *Dictionary of Jesus and the Gospels*, ed. Joel B. Green, Scot McKnight, I. Howard Marshall (Downers Grove, Ill.: InterVarsity, 1992), 86. As a source he cites the Midrash, Exodus Rabbah 46.1.

8. "It reflects the Jewish custom in which the formal wedding is preceded by a legally binding betrothal. During this period, which normally lasts no longer than a year, the pair were called husband and wife. To dissolve the betrothal required a formal divorce, which Joseph briefly considered doing with Mary (Matt. 1:18–20). As part of the betrothal, gifts were exchanged between the families. The bridegroom paid a bride-price to the family of the bride (Ex. 22:16–17), while the bride's father presented a dowry to his daughter (Judg. 1:14–15). When the wedding day arrived, the bride prepared herself by dressing in finery, such as an embroidered garment (Ps. 45:13–14), jewels (Isa. 61:10), ornaments (Jer. 2:32), and a veil (Gen. 24:65)." Mark Wilson, "Revelation," in *Zondervan Illustrated Bible Backgrounds Commentary*, ed. Clinton E. Arnold (Grand Rapids: Zondervan, 2002), 4:354.

Paul is not just preaching a set of abstract truths. He is not just presenting people with some philosophy. He is proclaiming the person of Christ, and through his preaching he is presenting that person to the congregation. "I have betrothed you to Christ," he says. "You are engaged to be His." Samuel J. Stone so beautifully says about the church:

> From heaven He came and sought her
> To be His holy bride;
> With His own blood He bought her,
> And for her life He died.

Christ has paid the bride-price for all believers. Therefore, we are legally and inalienably His. He is coming again for His bride, the church, to lead us home to His Father's house where He will present us spotless before His Father in heaven. There will be a wedding procession and festivities that will last not for a week or two, but for all eternity. We will be with Christ and behold His glory. The story of salvation is a love story. The covenant of grace is a marriage contract. Before the worlds were made, God the Father chose a bride for His Son and drew up a marriage contract between them. This wedding involves choice, not mutual attraction. God chose us in eternity and gave us to Christ, who bought us at Calvary and took us as His own through the preaching of the gospel; and now He will come back for us. When He comes back to claim us, we will enjoy intimacy and fellowship with Him forever.

The whole Trinity is involved in this marriage. The Father gives us His Son as our Bridegroom and gives us as a bride to the Son. As Ephesians 5:25 says, Christ purchased His bride with His blood and death. Ephesians 1:14 says the Holy Spirit is given to us as an *earnest* or guarantee. That guarantee, in ancient times, was shown by a down-payment. Today, this is commonly symbolized by an engagement ring. When Christ betroths us to Himself, He gives us the Spirit as a kind of engagement ring that guarantees that we shall arrive at the last day for the actual wedding.

James Hamilton puts it so well when he writes, "We can scarcely imagine the glory of that wedding day," noting that:

- Never has there been a more worthy bridegroom.
- Never has a man gone to greater lengths, humbled himself more, endured more, or accomplished more in the great task of winning his bride.
- Never has a more wealthy Father planned a bigger feast.
- Never has a more powerful pledge been given than the pledge of the Holy Spirit given to this bride.
- Never has a more glorious residence been prepared as a dwelling place once the bridegroom finally takes his bride.
- Great will be the rejoicing. Great will be the exultation. There will be no limit to the glory given to the Father through the Son on that great day.[9]

The invitation to this wedding feast is presented in Revelation 19:6–7: "Alleluia: for the Lord God omnipotent reigneth. Let us be glad and rejoice, and give honour to him: for the marriage of the Lamb is come."

The Bridegroom

The term *marriage of the Lamb* is strange because lambs don't get married. But Jesus Christ is presented here in His capacity as Savior. The Lamb of this marriage shows us His love by living for us and dying for us. He first appears as the Lamb in Revelation 5, where we read, "Thou art worthy to take the book, and to open the seals thereof: for thou wast slain, and hast redeemed us to God by thy blood out of every kindred, and tongue, and people, and nation" (vv. 6, 9). This love is a very one-sided affair, at least to begin with. "We love him," said John, "because he first loved us" (1 John 4:19).

When we think of the ideal marriage, we think of two lovers gazing into each other's eyes, starry-eyed with love. That is a Western view of marriage. It is different in many other parts of the world. There the parents of a bride often decide when she is to marry. In some cultures, she may have no say in the matter. She may not even know who her husband will be. She does not meet him until the day they are married. She learns to love him as her husband, and he

---

9. James M. Hamilton, Jr., *Revelation: The Spirit Speaks to the Churches*, Preaching the Word, ed. R. Kent Hughes (Wheaton, Ill.: Crossway, 2012), 351. Select statements from his paragraphs are taken and put in bullet point form.

learns to love her as his wife. We see this pattern, for example, in the marriage of Isaac and Rebekah (Gen. 24).

In some ways, that is the kind of marriage we have with Christ. We love Christ. But we only love Him because He loved us first. He loved us while we were yet sinners and were utterly unattractive and undeserving. He loved us while our carnal minds were still at enmity with Him. Our hearts were against Him, yet He loved us.

The prophet Hosea provides us with a powerful example of this love. God said to Hosea, "Go, take unto thee a wife of whoredoms and children of whoredoms: for the land hath committed great whoredom, departing from the Lord" (Hos. 1:2). That is what happened. As an adulteress, Gomer had a succession of affairs; and when her youth and attractiveness were spent, she ended up in the slave market. But Hosea found Gomer in the slave market and bought her back—not to exact revenge on her for the rest of her life, but out of sheer love (Hos. 3:2). He was a faithful husband to her despite her unfaithfulness to him.

That is how God loves you, dear believer, in Jesus Christ! When we were still sinners—unclean, unfaithful, adulterous, and promiscuous—He loved us. The apostle John said, "Having loved his own which were in the world, he loved them unto the end" (John 13:1). He loved them to the farthest limits of love.

We can't measure the length, breadth, height, and depth of the love of God; it surpasses knowledge. Jesus Christ loves us beyond our wildest imagination. He loved us all the way to the cross of Calvary. And there on that cross He paid the dowry to free us from the penalty of sin.

Sometimes when two people marry, one has a substantial bank account, and the other is in debt. But when they marry, they merge their accounts, for one flesh means one bank account. In a sense, that is similar to what Christ has done for us. When we were up to our necks in debt to a holy God because we had broken His law thousands of times, Christ took our liabilities and our debts and paid the price of all our sins. He was made sin for us. Christ became one flesh with His church. Her sins became His sins, and His perfect righteousness becomes hers through faith.

In his book, *The Best Match*, Edward Pearse seeks to allure sinners to come to Christ as their spiritual Husband. Like a good matchmaker,

Pearse extols the virtues of this Bridegroom who calls us to become His, and His alone. Do you want a match who has honor and greatness? He is God and man, the brightness of His Father's glory, the King of kings and Lord of lords. Do you want riches and treasures? Christ's riches are the best, for they last forever, are infinitely great, and will satisfy all your desires. Are you looking for a generous heart in a spouse? Jesus Christ is willing to lay out His riches for His spouse so that her joy may be full. Do you want wisdom and knowledge? The infinite wisdom of God shines in Him; He is Wisdom itself, and knows perfectly how to glorify Himself and do good to those who love Him. Are you looking for beauty? He is altogether lovely, more than all the beauty of human beings and angels combined. Are you seeking someone who will truly love you? Christ is love itself, love that is higher than the heavens and deeper than the seas. Do you want a husband who is honored and esteemed? This Husband is adored by the saints and angels. Everyone whose opinion really matters treasures Him; God the Father delights in Him. Do you seek a match who will never die and leave you a widow? Christ is the King immortal and eternal; He is the resurrection and the life.[10]

Behold the Lamb of God! Do you know Christ as the Lamb? Have you received Him as your heavenly Husband? Have you come to Him, repenting of your sin and throwing yourself on His mercy? Will you have Jesus Christ, the Son of God, to be your Savior, to love, honor, and obey, from this day forth and forever more? Will you have the Lamb of God to be your Husband—the Sin-bearer to be your Bridegroom? If you will have Him as your Bridegroom, you are invited to the marriage supper of the Lamb, but if you won't, you will not have Him at all.

The Bride

Revelation 19:7 records these words of the church triumphant: "Let us be glad and rejoice, and give honour to him: for the marriage of the lamb is come, and his wife hath made herself ready. And to her was granted that she should be arrayed in fine linen, clean and white: for the fine linen is the righteousness of saints." The bride asks, What shall I wear? What kind of raiment is fitting for someone who is to

---

10. Edward Pearse, *The Best Match: The Soul's Espousal to Christ*, ed. Don Kistler (Grand Rapids: Soli Deo Gloria, 2014), 56–70.

be married to such a Bridegroom? So she begins in earnest to seek those things that will honor and please Him. She seeks to be holy as He is holy, by His own sanctifying grace. She can't wait for the wedding. As the days go by, she checks off the days, counting how many are left before the big day. This is the picture you have here of the bride of Christ. She has made herself ready for the Bridegroom long before the wedding.

Paul speaks of this anticipation in 2 Timothy 4:6–8. He says, "For I am now ready to be offered, and the time of my departure is at hand. I have fought a good fight, I have finished my course, I have kept the faith: henceforth there is laid up for me a crown of righteousness, which the Lord, the righteous judge, shall give me at that day: and not to me only"—and then he widens it out to encompass every true believer—"but unto all them also that love his appearing." True Christians love Christ's coming, looking forward to that day with joyful anticipation and great longing.

Spurgeon said: "It ought to be a daily disappointment when our Lord does not come; instead of being, as I fear it is, a kind of foregone conclusion that he will not come just yet."[11] So are you longing for Christ's return? Here, through the preaching of the gospel, partaking of the Lord's Supper, in prayer meetings, and other spiritual disciplines, we see Christ, but through a glass darkly. We prize the means of grace, but how much more will we prize the day when we shall see Christ face to face!

What is most amazing is that Christ loves us and desires to be with us. As a pastor, I counsel young couples who can hardly wait to be married. One young man wondered aloud why he and his fiancée had set their wedding date so far in the future. Likewise, the Lord Jesus Christ yearns for His eternal marriage with His beloved bride. Psalm 45:11 says: "So shall the king greatly desire thy beauty." Dear believer, in His great love, Jesus Christ will beautify you now with His own image and holiness because He is looking forward to embracing you one day as His bride.

He is the King of heaven, and the King greatly desires you, for you will be lovely in His sight. The King of kings will make us His

---

11. C. H. Spurgeon, "Between the Two Appearings," Sermon of March 15, 1891, on Heb. 9:26–28, in *The Metropolitan Tabernacle Pulpit* (1892; repr., London: Banner of Truth, 1970), 37:155.

queen. He who rules over the whole universe will make us queen of heaven. The angels will be our servants. The King will take us by the hand and lead us to Paradise, His own personal garden, where we will live with Him forever!

Various stories tell about a great prince who marries a lowly maiden. But that is nothing compared to what we will one day experience when—wonder of wonders—the greatest Prince of all, the King of kings, takes the hand of us lowly creatures. That wonder immensely adds to the love and beauty and splendor of this astonishing heavenly marriage. It is truly the story that ends, "And they lived happily ever after."

We know both from the Bible and experience that marriage is the closest human relationship. The intimacy between a loving husband and a loving wife is beyond words, for the two indeed become one flesh (Eph. 5:31). But Paul speaks of an even greater mystery "concerning Christ and his church" (v. 32). In glory, dear believer, our closeness to Christ will far surpass even the intimacy between a husband and wife.

Due to being saved by grace alone from the enormity of our sin, our intimacy with the Lord Jesus Christ will be greater than what He experiences with the holy angels who have been with Him in perfect holiness for thousands of years. We will have a direct, personal, intimate, mystical union with the Lord Jesus Christ, which will allow no distance between us.

> When I in righteousness at last
> Thy glorious face shall see,
> When all the weary night is past,
> And I awake with Thee
> To view the glories that abide,
> Then, then I shall be satisfied.[12]

Ephesians 5:25 says that Christ purchased His bride with His death. The bride will also be beautifully adorned for her Husband (Rev. 21:2). In most weddings a bride wears a special gown, which she has chosen and paid for. But in heaven we do not have to purchase a wedding dress, for that dress is the gift of God's grace. Isaiah

---

12. *The Psalter, With Doctrinal Standards, Liturgy, Church Order, and Added Chorale Section* (Grand Rapids: Reformation Heritage Books, 1999), no. 31, verse 7 [Ps. 17:15].

61:10 says, "I will greatly rejoice in the LORD, my soul shall be joyful in my God; for he hath clothed me with the garments of salvation, he hath covered me with the robe of righteousness, as a bridegroom decketh himself with ornaments, and as a bride adorneth herself with her jewels."

The robe of righteousness that we wear on our glorious wedding day is the realization of our imputed blamelessness and holiness through Christ (Eph. 5:27), for He has redeemed us from sin's guilt and purifies us to be zealous for Him (Titus 2:14). So, this gown is the robe of Christ's perfect righteousness imputed to us in justification (2 Cor. 5:21). Christ takes off the filthy garments of our guilt and clothes us with the clean and beautiful clothing of His merit (Zech. 3:1–5). His obedience is credited to us. We read in Revelation 7:14 of countless people from every nation who "have washed their robes, and made them white in the blood of the Lamb." How did they wash their robes and make them white? By trusting in Christ alone for justification from the guilt of all sin. You can receive this cleansing only through faith—the self-abandonment of trusting Christ alone to make you acceptable to God.

Next, Christ continues to cleanse us from impurity in our sanctification. One day that sanctification process will be perfected and perfect holiness will be the gown that is given to us. Revelation 19:8 says, "And to her was granted that she should be arrayed in fine linen, clean and white: for the fine linen is the righteousness of saints." Literally, the Greek text says "the righteous deeds [δικαιώματά] of the saints." Thus getting ready for the day that Christ comes for you does involve effort on your part. We are told in verse 7 that "his wife has made *herself* ready." The man who says he belongs to Christ and yet never lifts a finger to purify himself is deceived. The Christian life means getting ready. It means putting off the old way of living and putting on the new.

As Paul says in Colossians 3:8–9, "But now ye also put off all these; anger, wrath, malice, blasphemy, filthy communication out of your mouth. Lie not one to another, seeing that ye have put off the old man with his deeds." Then verse 12 says, "Put on therefore, as the elect of God, holy and beloved, bowels of mercies, kindness, humbleness of mind, meekness, longsuffering." It is serious business to make ourselves ready for the return of Christ. There are no shortcuts, no secrets, and no easy escape routes. We have to *make ourselves ready*!

At the same time, this preparation is entirely a matter of grace. Notice here that "fine linen, clean and white...the righteousness of saints" (v. 8) is *given* to the bride to wear. You and I ought to be totally involved in the business of sanctification; yet, at the same time, sanctification is entirely a matter of grace. In short, the Lord reigns over His prepared bride, making her willing by His power! Verse 6 puts it this way, "Alleluia: for the Lord God omnipotent reigneth."

Christ reigns over every part of our salvation—even our sanctification. As Paul says in Ephesians 5:25–27, "Christ also loved the church, and gave himself for it; that he might sanctify and cleanse it with the washing of water by the word, that he might present it to himself a glorious church, not having spot, or wrinkle, or any such thing; but that it should be holy and without blemish."

A wrinkle or spot is a sign of age or disease. People spend a fortune to get rid of spots and wrinkles. We are told here that Christ is going to present His church without a single spot or wrinkle to His Father in heaven. He will come with all His holy angels and will take the church by the hand. He will lead her before God and the assembled hosts of the universe. In eternity He chose us. We do not know why. There is nothing in us to merit His choice. What is more, He bought us with His own blood at Calvary. And now He is beautifying us by the gospel and by His Holy Spirit.

As all the hosts of heaven look at the bride on her wedding day, they will give God all the glory. Verses 6–7 tell us: "And I heard as it were the voice of a great multitude, and as the voice of many waters, and as the voice of mighty thunderings, saying, Alleluia: for the Lord God omnipotent reigneth. Let us be glad and rejoice, and give honour to him: for the marriage of the Lamb is come, and his wife hath made herself ready."

The Guests Invited to the Supper

If the church is the bride, then who are the guests? Some have said that there will be at the wedding those who are married to the Lamb, and others who are just onlookers or guests. We need to remember that the language of Revelation is symbolic. This is the marriage of the Lamb, but of course lambs don't get married. When Jesus says in John 10, "I am the good shepherd," and then He says, "I am the door," you wonder how He can be both. But He is really more than that and all the other descriptions and designations in Scripture put together. In the same way, the church is the bride of Christ as well as the company of guests at the wedding.

Heaven is a place of festivity. You will be thoroughly and profoundly happy in heaven, for it is a place of everlasting happiness, celebration, and festivity. When we partake of the Lord's Supper, we remember that Christ Jesus accomplished complete salvation for us. The Lord's Supper, however, is only a foretaste of heaven's eternal supper (Luke 22:18). In heaven we will feast both with Christ and upon Christ.

In biblical times, sharing supper with someone was a sign of fellowship and closeness (Rev. 3:20). That's why the Pharisees were so upset with Jesus for eating with publicans and sinners (Luke 15:2). But what Jesus did makes the gospel accessible to us all. "Hallelujah— this Man receives sinners!" we cry out.

When Jesus invites needy sinners to the marriage supper, He offers us an experience of fellowship that is beyond words. The Bible says that when a couple gets married they are to leave their parents to enter into a new relationship. While they were children, the closest relationship the bride and groom had was with their parents. But now the closest relationship they have is with each other as husband and wife. That is the best metaphor to describe the relationship between Christ and His church. As we feast with Christ in heaven, we will have an intimacy that can only be compared to as that between a husband and wife—yet it far surpasses even that.

Unlike human marriage, there will be no sexual relations in heaven (Matt. 22:30). We will not have physical relations, but we will have an intimacy that is even deeper. We will have an eternal, perfectly pure relationship with the Lord Jesus Christ, far beyond anything here on earth. We will enjoy His embraces of love and will express our love for Him. There will be heavenly ecstasy without any sin or hindrance. It will be the purest, deepest emotion of love possible between the perfect Husband and the purified, perfected wife. When we are married to Jesus Christ, we will find our greatest delight in Him, and He will be delighted with us. Peter leaves us to ponder what this will be like since, as He notes, we already have such joy in Him: "Whom having not seen, ye love; in whom, though now ye see him not, yet believing, ye rejoice with joy unspeakable and full of glory" (1 Peter 1:8).

In his book, *Heaven Help Us,* Steve Lawson tells about a young aristocrat, William Monteague Dyke, who was stricken with blindness at the age of ten. The boy was very intelligent and went on to the university. While he was in graduate school, he met the beautiful daughter of a British admiral. The courtship soon flamed into romance. Though he had never seen this woman, William fell in love with the beauty of her soul. The two became engaged.

Shortly before the wedding, at the insistence of the bride's father, William agreed to have eye surgery that might or might not restore his sight. The doctors operated on William and bandaged his eyes. He was then confined to bed with his eyes covered with bandages until the wedding.

William requested that the bandages be removed from his eyes during the ceremony, just when the bride made her way down the center aisle. As the organ signaled for the bride to come down the aisle, every heart waited to see what would happen. As the bride came down the center aisle, William's father began to unwrap the gauze over his son's eyes. When the last bandage was removed, light flooded into William's eyes. Slowly, William focused on the radiant face of his precious bride. Overcome with emotion, William whispered, "You are more beautiful than I ever imagined."[13]

Something like that will happen to us when the bandages are taken away from our eyes, and we see Jesus. We will attain to what medieval theologians called the beatific vision, the very thing Christ prayed for when He said, "Father, I will that they also, whom thou hast given me, be with me where I am; that they may behold my glory" (John 17:24). Then we will worship our heavenly Husband forever. He will gaze upon us as His bride and see only beauty—His own work in us. He will see no sin. We shall be like Him and see Him as He is. We will be as perfect in soul and in body as He is. As 1 Corinthians 2:9 says, "Eye hath not seen, nor ear heard, neither have entered into the heart of man, the things which God hath prepared for them that love him." Hallelujah!

---

13. Steven J. Lawson, *Heaven Help Us! Truths about Eternity That Will Help You Live Today* (Colorado Springs: NavPress, 1995), 168–69.

Concluding Application

The Lord Jesus offers His hand in marriage to you. Will you receive it by faith and repentance? There is a sense in which everyone is called to this wedding. The gospel is to be preached to all creatures. God freely and lovingly invites *all* to this wedding. The invitations are out. All are welcome to come to Christ.

But to come to this wedding, you must be born again. You must know something of the marks of the Spirit's saving grace in your soul. You must know what it means to respond to God's overtures of salvation with true repentance and saving faith. You must learn of your need of the Bridegroom as your only hope of salvation. You must know something of your own depravity and something of Christ's marvelous deliverance from it. And you must want to live for Him in gratitude if you are going to sit at His table wearing His wedding garment. You must be prepared for this table by being stripped of your righteousness. You must long for the day of your eternal marriage with Christ.

I can't tell you how this world is going to end. But I can tell you that there will be a wedding, the wedding of all time, and you're invited! And the gospel demands a response from you—your R.S.V.P. As Paul says in Ephesians 5, "For this cause shall a man leave his father and mother, and shall be joined unto his wife, and they two shall be one flesh. This is a great mystery: but I speak concerning Christ and the church" (vv. 31–32). The gospel demands that you repent of your sin and cleave to this only Savior by true saving faith.

Those who do repent and trust in Christ can sincerely confess that their greatest hope is the hope of being with Christ and beholding His glory. David sings of this hope in Psalms 16:11 and 17:15: "Thou wilt shew me the path of life: in thy presence is fullness of joy; at thy right hand are pleasures for evermore.... As for me, I will behold thy face in righteousness: I shall be satisfied, when I awake with thy likeness." All who share this faith and cherish this hope can sing:

> The King there in His beauty,
> Without a veil is seen:
> It were a well-spent journey,
> Though seven deaths lay between:
> The Lamb with His fair army,
> Doth on Mount Zion stand,

And glory, glory dwelleth
In Emmanuel's land.

O Christ, He is the fountain,
The deep, sweet well of love!
The streams on earth I've tasted
More deep I'll drink above:
There to an ocean fullness
His mercy doth expand,
And glory, glory dwelleth
In Emmanuel's land.

Let me conclude with three practical lessons we can apply from this truth of Christ, the centerpiece of heaven, to whom we may one day be married in the greatest wedding of all time.

1. Since Christ is the jewel in heaven's crown—for He is what makes heaven *heaven*—strive to make Him the center of your life here on earth. You can get to heaven without money, education, beauty, or friends. But you cannot get there without Christ. Only those who are now engaged to Christ will one day be married to Him in heaven. So put all your energy into focusing on Christ in His person, names, natures, states, offices, and benefits.

2. As a bride prepares herself for her wedding, we must do likewise. The more we yearn for our marriage with Christ, the more we shall seek for that holiness without which no man shall see the Lord. But the less we think of it, the less we will follow the Lord Jesus in this life. During an engagement, those who are betrothed to each other are not allowed to court other people. We must not flirt with sin but push it far from us and say, "I will keep myself pure for the Lord Jesus Christ."

3. Remember that death will soon usher you into glory to forever be with your heavenly Husband. In John 14:2–3 Jesus says, "In my Father's house are many mansions: if it were not so, I would have told you. I go to prepare a place for you. And if I go and prepare a place for you, I will come again, and receive you unto myself; that where I am, there ye may be also." Death for believers is our gateway into His throne room, to see the beautiful face of our Lord and Savior and Bridegroom, Jesus Christ. Thus through all our lives and on our deathbeds we can sing:

Whom have I, Lord, in heaven but Thee,
To whom my thoughts aspire?
And, having Thee, on earth is nought
That I can yet desire.

Though flesh and heart should faint and fail,
The Lord will ever be
The strength and portion of my heart,
My God eternally!

CHAPTER 12

The Final Victory
(1 Corinthians 15)

Gerald M. Bilkes

Throughout the Bible we read of many battles, small ones, and great ones; battles lost and battles won. We love the accounts of the victories won by the people of God with the help of their God. Think of the victory of Israel at the Red Sea over Pharaoh and his host, or of David over Goliath, the champion of the Philistines. Another memorable victory was the victory over Sennacherib by the angel of the Lord, when 185,000 Assyrian soldiers were killed (2 Kings 19:35). But none of these victories, inspiring and God-glorifying as they are, can compare to the victory that Christ accomplished on the cross, where he defeated sin and Satan, and now proves that He has "the keys of death and hell" (Rev. 1:18). That victory of Christ on the cross is unpacking itself in the daily lives of Christians, as they fight against sin, Satan, and the world. Though we may feel defeated often, the Word of God assures believers that they are "more than conquerors through him" who loved them (Rom. 8:37). From out of Christ's one sacrifice for sin, there are daily victories for the people of God over sin. There is no doubt as to their overcoming by the blood of the Lamb (Rev. 12:11).

Yet, to our senses, there will be nothing quite paralleling the final victory, in which Christ's victory on the cross will bring all victories to a climax and inaugurate for the people of God something where never a skirmish, fight, or threat will enter, when the victory will be unpacked perfectly and entirely, forever. This truth ought to challenge and encourage all believers, as we see Paul doing in 1 Corinthians 15:24–58, in which, speaking of the end (v. 24), he mentions three "lasts": the last enemy (v. 26); the last Adam (v. 45b); and the last trumpet (v. 52).

The Last Enemy

One of the chief problems Paul had to address in his letter to the Corinthians was the belief some had that the future was already now. Through the influence of false teachers, some misunderstood the gospel to mean that if you were a Christian you had already passed into the fullness of life and that there was no future event called the resurrection (1 Cor. 15:12). The resurrection, so these people thought, was in the here and now, living at some higher plane on which you could live and enter into the fullness of life. For some it involved that they could live as they pleased because the judgment had kind of passed for them and they had their heaven on earth now (1 Cor. 15:32). They thought they might as well live it up now, because for them it was inconceivable that there would be a resurrection event in the future. To them the body was something despised and to be done away with.

"Not so," Paul countered. Christ rose with a physical body. Though Christians have, spiritually speaking, passed from death to life (1 John 3:14), there is a future, a glorious future, in which the resurrection of the body will take place. "Then cometh the end" (v. 24), Paul said to these people who imagined that the end had already come. It is as if he is saying: "What you have now, if you are a child of God, is special. It is the beginning of eternal life in your heart and life. It affects your walk and talk. It will show itself in holy living in all areas of life, but don't think that the end has already come and gone. For the end is still to come."

This is an important reminder for all of us. For though we have been taught the correct doctrine of the end of the world, and the resurrection of the body, and heaven and hell, many today still imagine that it is on *this* side of eternity that we ought to soak up as much pleasure and happiness as we can. This is true not only among those who espouse a health, wealth, and prosperity gospel. It is true of many who, with an orthodox doctrine in their creeds and confessions, still live under the spell of materialism, thinking that happiness is bound up with stuff—with things that we can taste, touch, and handle. There are others, both inside and outside the church, who try to live "at a higher plain," tapping into spiritual forces and consciousnesses that augment their sense of happiness, and they think *this* is life. The Corinthian spirit is alive and well in our Western world. Many "live it up" while forgetting *the end*, as the Word of God says loud and clear: "Then cometh the end."

One of the great reminders that there is an end is the truth about the "last enemy" (v. 26). Paul introduces us to him here in our text. We do well to remember that there are many enemies of God and of the soul. Sin is a great enemy. The devil is an ancient enemy, and a great one. The world is also a sly but terrible enemy. Our own sinful flesh is a very strong enemy. False doctrine, false prophets, and hypocrites are terrible enemies. Wicked governments are enemies of God and the soul. Persecutors of the faith are enemies. Every unconverted person is an enemy of God. So there are many enemies. Yet, by His resurrection, Christ has power and authority over every enemy. None can win against him. He is putting all His enemies under His feet, without exception (Heb. 2:8). He does not do it all at once. He does it over time, throughout world history even since His ascension. Psalm 110:1 records how the Father says to the Son: "Sit at my right hand until I make thine enemies thy footstool." The enemies are being destroyed one by one. A false teacher arises and Christ allows him to show his enmity, but then, Christ shows His power, unmasking the lies. And one by one He brings them into eternity to stand before Him. Kingdoms come and kingdoms go. There are many dictators and governments that persecute Christ and His people, and Christ lets them go on ever so long, but then they come under His feet: communism, Islam, secularism, Hitler, Stalin, Mao Zedong, and all those who resist God and reject His Son. Every day that goes by, enemies are being dealt with, and one by one they are judged and consigned to outer darkness by the glorious Son of God.

There is, however, an enemy who alone bears the name "last enemy." Christ allows him to go on the longest. Believers, you have suffered at the hand of this enemy, haven't you? Death is not a friend, no matter what society is trying to lure us into its attempts to legalize active euthanasia. When death takes your loved one, you feel the pain and hurt. There is grief for a long time. This enemy is merciless and cruel. He strikes older ones and young people. He is a terrible enemy, and he seems to have free rein. Why is this so?

Think of this parallel. Many military generals will keep back their fiercest brigade for the last segment of their struggle. They will hold these veterans in reserve, and call for them when everything else has failed. So too does Satan. This last enemy came on the scene first at creation, and he has devoured the whole human race with only a few exceptions: Enoch and Elijah — the third exception being Christ, of whom we are speaking. Unlike Enoch and Elijah, Christ did not escape death by being glorified instantly. No, Christ "died for our sins according to the Scriptures" (1 Cor. 15:3). Through death, however, He defeated this last enemy, having tasted death for every one of His people, and delivers us from death and the fear of death (Heb. 2:9–15). Because of that, even today, death must serve the purposes of Christ. Though he is the last enemy, he can only do Christ's bidding. And then, at the end, that last enemy "shall be destroyed" (v. 26). Think of that reality. Imagine that sight! Though death came into the world on the heels of our sin, we will see him destroyed. Death will die! What it did to others, it will suffer itself. Death will be destroyed by the power of the risen and ascended Savior.

Savor that little word "last." A last enemy! Yes, he is fierce, but he is final. He is large, but he is last. His sting is already gone. The sting of death is sin, and the power of sin is the law (1 Cor. 15:56). But then he will be destroyed before the eyes of all.

Remember, child of God, that you are risen with Christ and that neither death nor life is able to separate you from the love of God in Christ Jesus (Rom. 8:38–39). We don't need to fear death like the unconverted should fear death. Already now, people of God, Scripture says that death is "yours" (1 Cor. 3:21–22). You are not his, but he is yours. He is in the covenant of God, which is ordered in all things and sure (2 Sam. 23:5). Christ has made death a passage way into everlasting life (Answer 42 of the *Heidelberg Catechism*). One day your eyes will see death itself destroyed. Death will itself suffer defeat forever. It is no wonder the Bible says, "Wherefore comfort one another with these words" (1 Thess. 4:18).

If you are not in Christ, death is your enemy as well. Death is not your friend, my dear unconverted friend. It is a wage for sin (Rom. 6:23). What will it be to be destroyed with death at the end, which is not annihilation, but everlasting dying and never having any possibility to live again. What you experience when a loved one dies you will experience times infinity without hope, without respite, without a second chance. Don't believe Satan's lies. Death is no serene state that will mark the end of all troubles. No, your real trouble will only be just beginning and never ending.

This victory over the last enemy outstrips any victory in the Old Testament, and it makes us ask the question: Who is the champion? Who has secured this? Paul hastens to focus on Him next.

The Last Adam

Paul has been proving to the Corinthians not only that there will be a resurrection, but also how it will take place. We read in verse 35, "But how are the dead raised up? And with what body do they come?" In order to lift the veil on the mystery of how this all will happen when the end comes, Paul takes us back to creation.

Remember the creation of the first Adam. When God made him from the dust of the earth, He breathed into him the breath of life, and he became a living soul (Gen. 2:7). What an amazing and glorious creature Adam was when he was formed. He was strong and healthy. He was innocent and diligent. He communed with His Maker in the cool of the day. He knew God in righteousness and holiness. There was no spot of sin on him. How the angels must have rejoiced to see the image-bearer of God delighting in the glory of the triune God—Father, Son, and Spirit! That was the first Adam, and we were in him, federally represented by Him. We also are the genetic posterity of Adam and Eve, all 7.5 billion of us and counting. Everyone that has ever lived has descended from Adam. We are so used to hearing this, but what an amazing reality this is!

Have you learned what the truth of who you are in the first Adam means for you? In him, we sinned. We broke the covenant, and turned from God. We fell in the first transgression in Adam, and because of that fall, we walk after the course of this world, performing the lusts of the flesh (Eph. 2:1–4). All the Bible says about sin and iniquity applies to us because we are in Adam. And if we remain in Adam, we will die in our sins. In Adam, the law curses us; hell is open to us; and God is against us.

When we consider all this, what a mercy it is that there is even a second Adam. He was born of a virgin, without the involvement of man (Matt. 1:18). Because of that, He did not have the iniquity of Adam imputed to Him. Instead, He was the great, second, and last Adam. The first Adam died and we in him. The last Adam was Christ and He has come to raise the dead. "The first Adam was of the earth, earthy; the second Adam is the Lord from heaven" (1 Cor. 15:47). This second Adam was holy, harmless, and undefiled (Heb. 7:26); and yet He was made a sinless sacrifice and substitute, that He might not only undo what Adam did, but grant more, even everlasting life. As is the man of heaven, so are they who are of heaven. Those who are merely as they were born cannot inherit the kingdom of heaven; but those in Christ will bear the image of the heavenly (1 Cor. 15:49).

If you are still with the first Adam, you may indeed live for some time. You will live your earthly life and go about your appointed days; but nothing else. Then comes the end, and you will go into the place where all those who have lived and died with old Adam go, into outer darkness.

The final victory belongs only to those united to Christ, the Lord of heaven. They are made alive by Him (Eph. 1:4), and they are being transformed even now from one degree of glory to another, even by the Spirit of the Lord (2 Cor. 3:18). There is only defeat for those in Adam; but for those in Christ, and because of Him, there can only be victory. He is the Last. There is no other way. And His name shall endure as long as the sun and moon forever (Ps. 72:17).

Some reading this, convicted of their sins and state, might think, "There is no hope for me. I am lost and dead in trespasses and sins." But Paul gives much hope for sinners. He says that Christ was made "a quickening (or life-giving) Spirit" (1 Cor. 15:45) That means that Christ makes sinners alive. He not only died the death of His people, but He rose again. This last Adam can breathe upon slain sinners and they shall live. You need to look away from any and all, and look only to the second Adam. We need to rest in His finished work by believing the record God gives concerning His Son (1 John 5:10–11). It's the only way to overcome and be spared from spiritual and eternal death.

The first Adam brought in the last enemy; but the last Adam will destroy the last enemy. The first Adam brought defeat; the second, victory. The first brought the battle; the second won the battle. The first Adam forfeited heaven. The second Adam is the Lord of heaven. The first Adam brought death; the second Adam is life itself, and all that He has won will be revealed at the Last Trumpet (1 Cor. 15:52).

The Last Trumpet

Trumpets are glorious instruments! Because of its loud and commanding tone, the trumpet in the Bible was associated with warfare and with victory. Trumpets were sounded to gather people, and especially muster troops for battle (e.g., Zeph. 1:16).

This is exactly what Scripture prophesies regarding Christ's return. The angels will rally for a final battle, but it will be over in an instant. There will be no resistance. As when Gideon's trumpet sounded in the night and the enemy offered no resistance but turned on itself (Judg. 7:19–23) — so too will this trumpet mark the beginning of the battle as well as its end. All the ransomed will go to glory; all the wicked to eternal punishment. This is the first significance of the reference to trumpets at the end.

Second, trumpets in the Bible were used to mark fulfillments of God's decrees. In the book of Revelation, the trumpet sounds every time another of God's purposes is unfurled. Now, the last of God's decrees will be performed, and the trumpet will sound one last time. What has happened will forever stand — never to be reversed! Nothing will be undone ever again. Satan is forever defeated. God's people are forever raised incorruptible, unalterably alive; corruption has put on immortality. Everything will be final and unchangeable.

At the sound of the last trumpet, the graves will be opened, and the books will be opened (Rev. 19:11–15). Bodies will be joined again, each to its own soul and souls to their own bodies. The great white throne will appear and everyone will stand before it. Each shall give an account.

Is the trumpet already in the hand of the angel? Is he lifting it to his lips even now? Much like today, this final day will begin in a very ordinary way, but it will end like no other day has. If you are still in your sins when that trumpet sounds, what terror it will strike in you! Then Paul's words, "Then cometh the end," will be terrible words and introduce a terrible reality. This will mark the end of all entreaties. This will be the end of all hope of change. This will mark the end of all preaching, and the end of all possibility of being saved.

If you had already been in the grave, and your soul in hell, your body and soul will meet each other again, and irreversibly and eternally, you will be in torments. Should this truth not bring you to your knees?

What a glory, dear believer, this trumpet will inaugurate for you! Then Paul's words, "Then cometh the end" (1 Cor. 15:24) will introduce such good news. It will mark the end of all strife; the end of all sin; the end of all uncertainty; the end of all unbelief; the end even of one aspect of faith, for faith will be exchanged for sight.

Conclusion

This is the final victory. There is a final victory. It is the victory over the last enemy and all enemies. It is all because of the last Adam, the life-giving Spirit, and the Lord from heaven. It is all revealed at the last trumpet blast, which will mark the unalterable state of glory. Our understanding of it falls short, but we know enough, for God will be "all and in all" (1 Cor. 15:28). That's enough for believers. He will be the supreme, glorious, splendid, majestic, and adorable triune God—Father, Son, and Spirit. Time is hurling on steadily towards this end: reading this chapter was a blip on the timeline toward it. And it's about God, our All-and-in-All. Bend your knees before Him, and cast your all upon Him before it is forever too late.

Contributors

MICHAEL BARRETT is Vice President for Academic Affairs/Academic Dean and Professor of Old Testament at Puritan Reformed Theological Seminary. He is an ordained minister in the Heritage Reformed Congregations.

JOEL R. BEEKE is president and professor of Systematic Theology and Homiletics at Puritan Reformed Theological Seminary, a pastor of the Heritage Reformed Congregation in Grand Rapids, Michigan, and editorial director of Reformation Heritage Books.

GERALD BILKES is Professor of New Testament and Biblical Theology at Puritan Reformed Theological Seminary. He serves as an ordained minister in the Free Reformed churches.

DAVID P. MURRAY is Professor of Old Testament and Practical Theology at Puritan Reformed Theological Seminary. He serves as an ordained minister in the Free Reformed churches.

ADRIAAN C. NEELE is director of the doctoral program and professor of Historical Theology at Puritan Reformed Theological Seminary, research scholar at the Jonathan Edwards Center at Yale University, and is an ordained minister in the Heritage Reformed Congregations.

GREG SALAZAR is an assistant professor of Historical Theology at Puritan Reformed Theological Seminary. He also serves as a ruling elder at Harvest Orthodox Presbyterian Church, Wyoming, Michigan.

DAVID STRAIN is Senior Minister of First Presbyterian Church in Jackson, Mississippi.

DEREK THOMAS is the Senior Minister at First Presbyterian Church (ARP) in Columbia, South Carolina. He is also a Chancellor's Professor at Reformed Theological Seminary, and a Teaching Fellow with Ligonier Ministries.

DANIEL C. TIMMER is professor of Biblical Studies for the PhD program at Puritan Reformed Theological Seminary. He is an ordained ruling elder in the Reformed Church of Quebec and also serves at the Faculté de théologie évangélique in Montreal.

WILLIAM VANDOODEWAARD is Professor of Church History at Puritan Reformed Theological Seminary. He is an ordained minister who has served as a church planter.